Collected Poems

JUDITH MATHIESON

Order this book online at www.trafford.com
or email orders@trafford.com

Most Trafford titles are also available at major online book retailers.

Printed in the United States of America.

ISBN: 978-1-4269-3505-3 (sc)
ISBN: 978-1-4269-3506-0 (hc)
ISBN: 978-1-4269-3507-7 (e-b)

Library of Congress Control Number: 2010909202

*Our mission is to efficiently provide the world's finest, most comprehensive book publishing
service, enabling every author to experience success. To find out how to publish your book, your
way, and have it available worldwide, visit us online at www.trafford.com*

Trafford rev. 06/29/2010

 www.trafford.com

North America & international
toll-free: 1 888 232 4444 (USA & Canada)
phone: 250 383 6864 ♦ fax: 812 355 4082

Dedication

This book is dedicated to Life and all those people whose lives have touched mine.

PART ONE

PART ONE

TIME

The seconds tick by
Soon a moment is gone
Was it filled with a sad or a happy song?
Sometimes I don't give all that I'm capable of
Sometimes I hold back just a little bit of love.
The minutes turn into days
They fly by too fast
I do my very best to make those happy songs last
I can't help it though
Sometimes a negative thought creeps into my head
Then it's too late - angry words have been said.
Days beget weeks
They are too soon behind me
Did I change my circumstances?
Did I just let them be?
Am I striving to improve with each new day?
Am I being a little friendlier to those who come my way?
Weeks become months
Twelve make a year
Did I learn anything?
Did I lose any of my fear?
Some dreams came true, a few challenges were won
Was there anything still left undone?
There's always next year
Why wait till then?
Won't it just get lost in the shuffle of my thoughts again?
Why not do it now?
Do it right this very minute

Live life
Love life
Enjoy life
Challenge life
Learn from life
Listen to life
Do all of these things before it's too late.

LIVE LIFE

There's a stage in life we all go through
When we look back on what we've accomplished
When we look forward to the things we yet want to do
Time is soon lost in the abyss
Nobody knows how much time is left.
We must take our life into our own hands
We must not let it fly by unused
We must make it our own somehow
Let the past go
What's done is done
You can't change it one iota
In the future take a stand
Life is meant to be lived
It's meant to be lived now.
Time keeps passing by
Why are you still sitting here?
You know what you want to do
Sometimes you have to take chances
Sometimes you'll get hurt.
Life is passing by one second at a time
You might get left behind
That wouldn't be a good thing
Challenge life and enjoy life and use life
Yes, do these things while there is still time
Use your body and use your mind
Use your spirit too
Don't you know that there is no one else like you?
Don't hide any longer

Go out

I say go out!

Go out and sing your song to the world.

THIS FEELING

What is it that makes me feel this way?
It's more than spring fever
More than the first robin's song
More than the roses blooming in the garden
I feel it in the summer too
When I gaze at the magnificent sky above me
At the countless stars and the moon
In autumn it is there
As I watch the leaves change colour
When I'm out walking in winter
Listening to the crunch of snow beneath my feet
It hits me again
This feeling is still there deep inside of me.
I know what it is:
It's the feeling of being in love
Knowing that I'm loved in return
It didn't come in a rush, this feeling
No, it didn't.
It crept into my heart little by little
Until I knew that I had found my special someone
I knew that I had found my soul mate
I knew that I had found my man.

GO FOR IT! (1)

Why be so serious when things get you down
You make matters worse by wearing a frown.
Nobody is perfect
We all make mistakes
What does it matter if you don't get the breaks?
Laugh at your daydreams
It will help if you do
Never stop searching for the mystery of you.
You have the power to change circumstances
It's all up to you
You'll have to take a few chances.
Don't bury your talent in the ground
You know that would be wrong
Keep on working at it
One day when you're not expecting it
One day it will become your song.
There's lots of competition
Try to follow through
Don't you yet know the truth?
Your best competitor is you.
It's time to get up
It's time to shake off the gloom
Sweep your doubts out the door with a big broom.

DIFFERENT PEOPLE (1)

How can you know how I feel unless you ask me?

How can you assume to know my thoughts?

What gives you the right to judge me?

Does it matter if my way of living is different from yours?

None of us is perfect

We all make mistakes

Each one of us looks at life differently.

We don't all follow the same path

Who is right and who is wrong?

Everyone we meet influences us

Each new adventure makes us grow

We love and we play

We work and we cry

We laugh and we learn

We survive.

I don't understand why we destroy our home

Why do we destroy our world?

We do we destroy the earth with pollution?

Why do we abuse life, our most precious gift?

Why can we not accept ourselves as we are?

Why can we not accept others as they are?

I don't know.

Do you know?

We could learn from each other, couldn't we?

IT'S OUR LOVE

It's our love that keeps us together
It's our love that makes us strong
It's our love
It's you and me forever
It's our love
It's our special song.
It's your arms that enfold me
They're my shelter from the storm
Do you know what you do to me when you hold me?
I've found a place that's safe and warm.
No matter where we go in life
No matter what road we choose
Whether there's happiness or whether there's strife
With our love we just can't lose.
The past is gone
Its song has been long since sung
Mistakes were made and lessons were learned
This very moment has just begun
Its bridges haven't yet been burned.
It's our love that keeps us together
It's our love that makes us one
It's our love
Let's keep it forever
It will last no matter what comes.

THOUGHTS ABOUT CHRISTMAS

Christmas is the Birthday of God the Son
For all of humankind He became a little One
He was born to save us from our sins
He was born to lead us all back to His Father again.
Santa Claus comes only once a year
Jesus our Saviour is always near
He has gifts of Mercy and Love
He has all good things from Heaven above.
If we would open our hearts to Him
If we would let Him guide our lives
Then like King Solomon of old
Indeed we would be very wise.
Material things are given us for our pleasure
They add enjoyment to our lives
Let us not make them our only treasure
They are not are true treasure
Our true treasure is in Heaven.
Life is a beautiful gift from God
Happiness is a state of mind
Yet day by day we are destroying our world
We are making peace so difficult to find.
Peace must begin in people one by one
Like the rising and setting of the sun
Like the dawning of each new day
We must let Jesus lead the way.
Then the feeling would become so strong
More and more people would join in the song
Let's love not hate, let's give not take

The earth was given into our care
Let's make sure everyone has his or her share.
Listen people!
Yes, listen!
The Christmas Spirit should last all year round
Good feelings and deeds have a chance to abound
The tidings the Angels sang that first Christmas Day
They would in our hearts and minds forever stay.

EASTER TIME

Another Easter time is here
It's a very special time of year
Different though your thoughts may be
I'll tell you what it means to me.
Spring is on the way and new birth is everywhere
Again God shows us how much He really cares
The Child born at Christmas is now a Man
The wood from His Cradle is now a Cross
It's the Cross of humankind's salvation.
On the day that Jesus died
How many of His friends stood by and cried?
Not very many
How could they possibly do as He had asked?
They couldn't just then
They had to wait until three days had passed.
God's own Holy Spirit set them free
He can do the same for you and me
Take us away from our prison of sin
Show us how to live and how to love again
Why, oh why, oh why won't we let Him in?
How can we love our fellow man if we don't try to understand?
Do we see the tears in another's eyes when we too harshly criticize?
If we changed our thought process would we hate a little less?
Why don't we help others more when they stumble?
Why don't we let God's Holy Spirit touch us?
He will touch us like the warm wind in spring
Why don't we let Him teach us the right way to go?
Why don't we let him touch our hearts and our minds?

Why don't we let Him fill us with His Love?
Why don't we let Him fill us with His springs of living water?
He is standing at the door of our hearts
He is waiting so patiently
All we have to do is to open the door.

BLOOMING

God is great and God is good
He brought us together when the time was right
He knew when the time was right for us to fall in love
That's what we did
We fell in love
We shared our dreams and we conquered our fears
We sank our roots into fertile soil
Stretched our limbs with work and our minds with knowledge
Reached out for the sunlight of each new dawn
We felt the warmth of our love as it bloomed
Every day it bloomed stronger.

GIFTS

What is it that makes me feel this way?
Is it listening to the birds that sing?
Is it the fragrance of the flowers that bloom in May?
Is it watching a butterfly land on a flower?
Does my heart fly away only in spring?
No!
I feel the joy that the other seasons bring.
When the leaves turn to red and gold
When the ground is white with snow
I am enthralled by the beauty Nature shows.
On long summer nights when I look at the sky
Sometimes my eyes water as I praise God my Creator
I thank God for the gifts He has given to me.
Now He has given me another gift
Someone special to share my life with
A friend and a soul mate
A wonderful man
A husband to call my own
He knew it wasn't good to be alone.
For twenty years we've shared life's work and life's fun
Our two hearts, our two minds, our two lives became one
My love for you and your love for me
This is what gives me the feeling of ecstasy.

WHO AM I?

Oh Lord, who am I?
I am body, mind and soul
No matter how much time passes by
I'm still a unique individual
That much I know.
What is it that makes me unique?
Why do I act and feel the way I do?
Every thought I have
Every word I speak
Every dream I dream
They come from deep within me.
Still why am I here in this broken world?
This world so torn between good and evil
I'm here to use the talents that God gave me
To help someone ease their pain
To help someone smile again
That's why I'm here.
What do I do?
Where do I start?
I'll let the Holy Spirit lead the way
Tomorrow is another day.
What will I finally decide?
Is my dream all wrong?
Is it really worth working for?
Yes, it is!
Will I follow the wind?
Will I flow with the tide?
I will do my best and even more.

Where will this path lead?
I don't know.
What new people will come into my life?
Will they be full of fear?
Will they be full of fun?
Who can answer such a question?
Only time will tell
Only time will show me new faces
Only time will show me new places
Only time will teach me new experiences throughout the years.

RUMBLINGS

Ever since I met you
I've been happy with everything about you
Maybe I'm right or maybe I'm wrong
I choose you as my one and only
Together as we go through life
Happiness is what I wish for you and me.
Now and forever I'll always love you
In good times or bad times I'll always love you
I never want to make you sad
I just want to see your green eyes smile
Any time and any where I'll always love you
My love for you is always true.
Take my hand and walk with me
Stay with me throughout all eternity
Take my hand and take my heart
Take my all if it so pleases you
As long as I have you I'll never fall.
With you alone this love I'll share
I'll always love you
Forevermore I'll always care
For this love to you I give
Everything in life is worth nothing if you don't love me too
I hear you whisper that you do.
You and I will always be together for eternity
Take your hand and place it in mine
Together we'll be until the end of time.

I JUST WANTED YOU TO KNOW

I've been thinking about you and me
I've been thinking about us as time goes on
I've begun to realize just how much we've learned
I realize just how far we've come in a short time
We've come so far, so fast
We've come so fast, so far
Love has swept us off our feet
My love for you is growing and your love for me is growing
Our love for each other is growing
Our love is growing with every heartbeat.
It's difficult yet it's so wonderful
It's so wonderful to know that there's someone in my life
Not just anyone but a special someone
It's you!
You are my special someone.
Just thinking about you makes me smile
I think about you at home
I think about you while I'm working
Sometimes it brings a tear I'm not afraid to hide
Our time together is special
It is precious and beyond price.
This is the start of our journey
I never want our love's voyage to end
Except in the arms of my darling
You are my darling, you are my man
You are my lover, my husband and my best friend.

THIS PLACE

I came into this place last night
It didn't seem to be the same
I opened the door but no one came before me
No one gently whispered my name.
There were no boots on the mat
There were no glasses on the tray
Everything was left as if you'd just gone away
I entered the place and I felt your presence there
I called out to you as if you could hear
You didn't answer and I felt it, dear.
I read some and I watched some television
I listened to the radio too
They didn't mean anything to me
The thrill of my evening was my phone call to you
I heard your deep voice in this place of silence
It made me feel at peace.
Then came the hard part of settling down
I turned to that pillow beside me
I recalled the wonder, the thrill and the thunder
I felt love stir deep within me.
This place is empty
It's so full yet it's so empty
This place needs you, baby, and so do I
This place is where our love bloomed
This place is where we both swooned
This place is where we made love so tenderly for the first time.
This is our place
This is our space

We became one together in more ways than one
In this place we embrace again
Together we trace the growth of our feelings as we fell in love.

I AM NOT AFRAID

I am not afraid to say I love you!

I am not afraid to say I care!

I am not ashamed to say I need you

I wish that you were here beside me.

I am proud to say I want you

I will fight for us no end

I am happy to say that there is a "we"

Together we will overcome any obstacles waiting around the bend.

I am not afraid to say I love you!

I am not afraid to say how I feel inside

I want to shout it from the rooftops

My heart is bursting with love, with hope, with pride.

I am not afraid to say that my need to be near you is growing

My love for you is growing day by day

I pray for strength and courage and guidance

My love for you is here to stay

I am not afraid to say I love you!

YEAR'S END

Here we are again
Another year has ended
One lost a mother
The other a friend
It's time to reflect
It's time to lend
Our memories to the year again
Remember the Father
Think of the Son
Recall the year passed
Remember fears overcome
Spirit of Christmas
Spirit of Love
Spirit of Peace
Challenge us mortals
Lead us to your feast.

MY HUSBAND

My husband is the man to whom I said "I do!"
The man who told me he loves me too
The man who holds that special place in my heart
I knew this right from the very start.
The man who whispers in my ear
Words of love I alone should hear
The man in whose eyes love I see
I'm so glad that I found him and that he found me.
This man holds me all through the night
His smile greets me at morning's light
This man shares my love and my dreams
He shares my time and my prayers
I share his silly schemes.
This man understands my moods
I try to be patient with him too
The man whose wife I'm glad to be
We'll be together for eternity.

NIGHTMARE

I woke up screaming
I was having a bad dream
I just didn't understand
The things that I had seen
There was a knife in my hand
It was against my left wrist
I had no reason in the world
I had no reason to be doing this.
No, no, no, I yelled
I don't want to die
When the blood started to flow
It was too late to cry.

DAISY

My mother-in-law, Daisy, passed away
It was a year to the day after the towers fell
They were strong
They were part of New York's skyline
She was not at all well.
Terrorists destroyed the towers with a plane
Thousands of people died that day without warning
They had no time to say goodbye to their families and friends
Pulmonary fibrosis deteriorated her breathing
It took a few months
She died in her sleep early in the morning.
Memories of September 11, 2001
Memories of September 11, 2002
They will haunt me forever.

INNOCENT DREAMS

I don't feel like getting up this morning
I just want to lie here and dream
I want to dream the innocent dreams of a child.
Suddenly the thought went through my head
Like a river flowing red with blood
Not all children have innocent dreams
Some dream of war or violence or rape
Others dream of despair or cruelty or hate
Some others dream of gunfire in the night or stale bread
Not all children have innocent dreams
Will it always be so?
Will it ever change?

TIME AND A HOMELESS MAN

One day I was walking down the street
People were hurrying by
I didn't know where they were going and I didn't care
I also ignored the man who held out his hand
He asked for change to buy a coffee
I also passed him by
I had no time to stop then
I was on my way to meet my friend.
I'll give him something on the way back, I thought
I didn't know it would be too late
While my friend and I were enjoying a nice lunch
The homeless man had died
He had died alone
He had died cold and hungry
Call it the hand of fate
His time had come
For him it was the end.
A feeling of sadness descended on me
I said a prayer for his soul
I knew that he was with Jesus now
I knew now that he was whole.
What of me?
I didn't feel whole
I felt guilty
I could have bought the man a cup of coffee
I could have acknowledged him
He was a human being
I could have but I didn't

I had to meet my friend.
What was a minute or two out of my whole day?
It would have made a difference to him
Not so to my friend
She was late.

QUESTIONS

I lay in bed unable to sleep
I toss and I turn
My brain burns with questions I can't answer.
Can you?
Can anyone?
When will war end?
Will there ever be peace on earth?
When will violence and hatred cease?
When will the earth be green again?
When will trees and flowers grow undisturbed?
When will I see rivers with clear unpolluted water?
When will I breathe clear unpolluted air?
When will all people regardless of culture or lifestyle be friends?
Will there ever be peace?
Yes, there will be peace some day
It says so in the Bible
Meanwhile I must have faith
I must believe in God's Holy Word
I sigh and close my eyes
Sleep comes softly as a feather.

THE YEAR 2003 (1)

The past 365 days have been horrendous
They have brought heat waves
They have brought sinus headaches
Thousands of people in Europe died
There have been forest fires in California and British Columbia
There have been floods in Quebec.
People cried
They cried from frustration
They wept from exhaustion
Firefighters and other people worked diligently for days and nights on
end
They received a round of applause.
There were changing and weird weather patterns
There were green Christmases where white should have been
There were white Christmases in places where people had never seen
snow.
Then there was SARS
This was an extremely fatal lung disease
Dozens more people passed away
Others are still suffering today
Medical staff and volunteers everywhere were overworked
They tried to control the nasty bug
Thank God for their courage and their determination
Every one of them needs a hug.
There were earthquakes and mad cow disease
There were melting polar caps and blackouts
For many thousands of people it has been a year of sorrow
For numerous others a year of doubt

There were still wars in many parts of the world
There are still wars to this day especially in the Middle East
When, oh when will they ever learn?
When, oh when, will they tame the beast?
When, oh when will they ever learn?

HELLO

Hello, my love

Welcome home, my love

You've been away for a little while

I have really missed your smile

I hope you're feeling better, my love.

Please come in my love and close the door

Walk into my arms once more

They felt so empty when you weren't here

Everything felt wrong

Now it's all right, now you're back where you belong.

Touch me, my love

Turn my world upside down

Kiss me, my love

Make my world go spinning round

Every time our bodies or our minds or our spirits meet

I know that I am yours

I know that you are mine.

Deep down I hear it

Then my lips repeat it

I love you!

You are my husband

I am your wife

May it be so for the rest of our lives.

ODIN (1)

When he came into our lives
A five year old dog
We had no idea how much he would change us
He acted like a god.
He's a Golden Retriever
He's a gorgeous shade of red
We just can't get angry with him when he jumps up on the bed.
When he wakes me in the morning
Whining to go out
I get dressed in silence
Sometimes I want to shout.
When Odin's done his business
He wants to play in the snow
There's no way to resist those brown eyes
So the stick I throw.
When I come home after a busy day
He greets me with wagging tail
We can't leave him alone for long
His bark becomes a wail.
It seems we've had him forever
He fits in so well with us
There's no doubt he's our dog
He's part of the family.

JUST WAITING (1)

A teddy bear
He's just waiting to be bought
A book
It's just waiting to be read
A child
She's just waiting to be hugged
A lonely heart
It's just waiting to be touched.

ANOTHER DAY

Today is a brand new day
Another day for me to weep
Another day for me to sleep
I think I`ll go for walk with my husband instead
We can talk while Odin is having a run in the park.
Another day
Another twenty-four hours
What am I going to do with the time?
Am I just going to sit and sigh?
Am I going to turn my life around?
I`m going to visit a friend who`s housebound.
Another day to organize my books
Is that all I`m going to do?
Am I not going to learn something new?
How about learning how to cook or how to knit?
Well, maybe not those things
You never know though.
Another day
What a wonderful gift from God above
Another day to share a smile
Another day to light a stranger`s way
Another day to live
Another day to give back to God what He has given to us
Another day to help each other carry the heavy load
Sometimes it`s a very rough road.
Another day to laugh
Laughter can help smooth the path
Another day

Another evening's beautiful sunset
Thank you dear Lord above
Thank you for another twenty-four hours to love.

PART TWO

ODE TO AUTHORS(1)

Books surround me
They encircle the room
Which one will I choose?
I'll read a new one soon.
Murder mysteries
They make my blood run cold
Enchanting love stories
They bring back the knights of old.
Words of great mystics
They make my soul fly
Words that inspire me
Sometimes they make me cry.
Words on a page can take me to another place
They can even take me far away
They can even take me to the realms of outer space.
From the depths of their imagination
Storytellers write
They write whenever the muse strikes them
It could be day or it could be night.
Books make good friends
Anytime or anywhere
Books are a joy to read
They bring hours of pleasure
Thank you to all authors everywhere.

FOR MY HUSBAND

God keeps us in His tender care
He blesses the love that we two share
I try to show from day to day
I love you in every way.
Something happened from the start
You did something to my heart
You bring out the best in me
You set my mind and spirit free.
Even after all these years
My heart beats faster when you are near
No matter how much time goes by
You're still the apple of my eye.

EASTER BUNNY

This is for you my forever honey
This is from your Easter bunny
Love will be forever grand as long as by your side I stand
We'll share our joys and we'll conquer our fears
We'll wipe away each other's tears
We'll share our smiles
We'll make each moment alive with song
We'll find a place where we belong
We'll work together as a team
We'll try to capture our special dream
We'll continue to walk hand in hand
Through this big and wonderful land
We'll help others where we may
There will be times when things won't go our way
There will be times when all we can do is frown
Still we'll trudge along the road
We'll help each other carry the load
Sometimes we'll need help from others too
I know that won't be okay with you
I know you're a very independent man
I am independent too
We'll just accept it with a smile
Stay and rest a little while
Soon we'll be ready to move on
We'll sing our own heartfelt song.

A BIRTHDAY POEM

Happy Birthday to you, my love
You make my life complete
No one else will ever do
It's you who makes my life so sweet.
Another year
Another birthday
You've come through much illness
You've let God's love and our love heal you
Now it's a happy time
Now it's time to celebrate
You know I'll always love you
You'll always be in my heart and in my soul
You'll always be in my thoughts
You'll always be in my prayers.

HEAT WAVE

I'm lying on my bed
I'm trying to sleep
It's too hot to sleep
It's so hot and so humid
I have an aching head
Sweat runs in rivulets down my back
I get up and walk to the kitchen
I take an extra-strength Tylenol for my sinus headache
I return to the bedroom
The fan is on low
I turn it to medium
When, oh when will this heat wave end?
This is the fifth day
When, oh when will it go away?
The sun smiles and laughs
He's saying not yet, my friend, not yet.
It's hot
It's so damn hot
It's so damn humid
It's so damn hot and so damn humid.
The grass is brown
The flowers are all wilted
The people are all wilted too
When will it rain?
We're so thirsty
We're begging for water
Just before I close my eyes I ask again
When will it rain?

Nobody answers.
Two more days passed
Three elderly people died from the high humidity
Something woke me up in the wee hours of the morning
It was raining!

SIDEWAYS FALL

I remember the day it happened
It seems like yesterday but it was much longer than that
It was five years ago when my husband fell and broke his leg.
His femur was shattered
He turned white with pain
A fireman gave him oxygen
He was almost unconscious by then.
The paramedics arrived
They took him to a hospital in Etobicoke
We didn't live anywhere near there
It was the only place to go.
The operation lasted two-and-a-half hours
I prayed and I waited
I prayed some more
I waited some more
The nurse finally let me see him
He was well sedated.
I whispered softly I love you
I'll see you tomorrow
I don't know if he heard me or not
I had an hour-and-a-half bus ride home
It was after ten-thirty when I arrived
I didn't cry
I fought the tears.
He was alive!
Nothing else mattered
He now had two pins and four screws in his left leg
It didn't matter

He was alive.
I knew he would be all right and he was
He spent two weeks in the hospital
He spent a month in rehabilitation
Then he came home
He was home!
He was home at last
Thank You, Lord Jesus!
Thank You!

DEEP FREEZE

Canada is in a deep freeze
From the Maritimes to Ontario
The wind howls and blows fiercely
The temperature drops and keeps on dropping
It's even too cold to snow.
Finally the wind calms down
The temperature rises to ten below
The next morning I look out of the window
The ground is covered with snow.
I take Odin for a run in the park
He loves the snow and acts like a puppy
The park is full of people and their pets
Odin ignores them all and chases his Frisbee.
The next day is sunny but cool
There's no wind chill in sight
It's a beautiful day for walking and a beautiful day for shopping
The temperature takes a dive that night.
Forty-five below with the wind chill factored in
Odin whines to go out
He doesn't waste any time
He dislikes the cold.
The deep freeze lasts for a week
People only go outside for emergencies
On Saturday I wake up to a surprise
The sun is shining through the window
It's a balmy minus five degrees.

MY GUARDIAN ANGEL

My Guardian Angel is always beside me
She watches over me during the long nights
When the dawn breaks she stays
She doesn't take flight.
She's by my side during the day
She protects me from harm
When I stumble she's always there
She gently takes my arm.
When my life is full of joy
She shares my happiness
She knows that Jesus fills my heart with love
My husband, my special friend, my dog
She knows they fill my heart with bliss.
When my life is full of pain
She walks with me every step of the way
You'll get through this, she whispers
Everyone needs a little rain.
There have been times in my life
When I've gone far astray
With tender patience she leads me
She leads me back
She puts me on the right path again.
Even though I can't see her
I know she's always there
She guides my steps
She guards me with strength, with love and with care.

OUR TRIP TO PERU

My husband and I were talking the other day

"Where do you want to go on vacation this year?" he asked

"Peru," I replied.

Before the month was done we had all our shots

Ouch!

We received the necessary travel documents in the mail

Odin, our Golden Retriever, knew that something was up

He whined as if to say what about me?

The lady who grooms Odin agreed to look after him while we were away

Now he's happy.

Departure day arrives

We fly to New York and on to Miami

From Miami we fly to Lima

We're in Peru

Finally!

We meet the rest of the group

Two more couples from Canada

Two couples from England

A couple from Holland

The time disappears way too fast.

We see new sights and we hear new sounds

We smell and we taste new food

All of our senses are heightened:

The culture, the people and the scenery

It's all so incredible.

The pre-Inca ruins, the Nazca Lines

The Sacred Valley of the Incas

The spectacular view from Machu Picchu
There's so much to see
It's so difficult to take it all in.
The knowledge that these people had is amazing
Where did they receive such knowledge?
Who gave it to them?
Knowledge about geometry
Knowledge about agriculture
Knowledge about the cosmos
Does anyone know?
There are all kinds of assumptions but nobody really knows.
Now it's time to leave this beautiful country
This country so full of mystery
I'll never forget the experience
I'll never forget what it has taught me.

THINKING

I'm sitting in my apartment and thinking
I'm thinking about the past
That's really silly, isn't it?
I know that it couldn't last
It's gone
It's gone forever
It's sunk into the abyss of time.
I think about childhood games of tag and hopscotch
Games of hide-and-seek and jumping rope
Just like my friends from school only the memories remain.
Teenage years are now far behind me
New ideas have entered my head
Shopping for clothes, high school dances, the thrill of my first kiss
They have all disappeared.
College days and jobs
The people I met along the way
People I have helped
People who have helped me through bad times
Some have moved on to new adventures
Sad to say though some have gone
It's true that the past is no more
It did what it was supposed to do
It helped me to grow and to learn
It helped me to survive
It has made me the woman I am today.
Now at this moment I'm still sitting here
I'm listening
I hear the clock chiming

The rain beating on the window pane
The wind whispering softly in the trees
My husband's steady breathing
He sighs.
Someone down the hall laughs
A dog barks and a baby cries
A phone rings and a man shouts.
I look at the possessions surrounding me
Pictures hanging on the wall
Teddy bears and dolls placed throughout the room
A computer, a television, a radio or two
A microwave
The records, the videos, the CD's
The books
Oh, the books!
Middle-aged now I play with different toys
I play a whole new set of games
What will they all mean in the scheme of things to come?
Will any of them matter tomorrow?
No, not one of them will matter tomorrow.

KEEP IT SIMPLE (1)

Keep it simple.

Three little words

Three simple little words

Simple yes, but so difficult to do in this world of war

This world of terror

This world of violence

People are confused and frustrated

They don't know who to believe

They don't know who to trust.

People are anxious

They are stressed out

Some use drugs and alcohol and sex

They hope that these false gods will ease their pain

It's only a temporary solution.

Some commit suicide and end it all

They will never see another sunrise

They will never again hear a child's laughter.

Pre-teen gangs wander the streets with knives and guns and any other weapons they can find

They do violence

They destroy property

They hurt people

They don't know who to believe

They don't know who to trust.

Keep it simple.

Is such a thing actually possible in this present world?

Is it?

Is it?

Why is war still raging in the land where Jesus once walked?
Bodies of wounded soldiers lie on the ground
The bodies of innocent victims lie beside them
Bodies of the dead are everywhere.
Blood and guts are everywhere
Another suicide bomber explodes
She kills and maims dozens
People are so full of anger and rage and hate
They don't know who to believe
They don't know who to trust.
Keep it simple.
What do you think?
Will the humankind of this world really do that one day?
Will we finally get it right?
Will we finally see the light?
Will we learn to keep things simple?
Will we learn to live in peace as God intended us to do?
When will this beautiful event happen?
Only when we learn to trust God
Only when we learn to believe in God's Holy Word
It's only then will this beautiful event happen.

BLESSINGS

I woke up one morning feeling blue
That day I did nothing except lie in bed
My thoughts were terribly depressing
Is this all there is?
Why hang around?
Life is futile
Life is so absurd
Life is so cruel sometimes I might as well end it.
Then I heard a voice
The voice said to count my blessings.
Was the voice in my head?
Was it on the radio?
It didn't matter
I did as the voice said and counted my blessings.
There were many of them
Some I took for granted
My health I had
Sometimes it was very good, at other times it was only fair
My husband was also my best friend
He was my lover and my confident
We shared a nice one-bedroom apartment
Odin, our Golden Retriever, made three
He filled our lives with joy and laughter.
There's more!
I had my eyes to see my husband's smile
My eyes saw flowers in the spring
They saw birds on the wing
They saw raindrops

They saw the stars of night
They saw every dawn's first light.
I had my ears to hear my husband's voice
My ears also heard beautiful music
They heard Odin barking
They heard waterfalls flowing.
I had my two arms to hold my husband
I had my two legs to walk with him.
I'm not done yet!
All the organs inside my body are so delicately balanced
God made me that way
They work together but each one had its own specific role.
That's a blessing, is it not?
Yes, indeed!
It most certainly is a blessing.
I have my father and my mother
I have my sister and my brother
My friends – the few friends I have – are good friends
They are true friends.
Even my material possessions are blessings.
My books, my computer, my collection of teddy bears and dolls
My clothes
My photograph albums
My television, my records, my CD's
All these things are blessings
They bring me pleasure.
There's one more thing
It is last but it is certainly not the least
In fact it is the most important blessing of all
Jesus loves me.

I know now that it was His Voice that I heard inside my head
It was His Voice that told me to count my blessings.
I'm so glad that I listened to His Voice.

MARY, JOSEPH AND JESUS (1)

Her name was Mary

She was a teenager, a young Jewish girl from Nazareth

One day something absolutely incredible happened to Mary.

The Archangel Gabriel came from Heaven

He had some awesome news for her

She would bear a Son but still remain a virgin

She asked Gabriel a question

She listened intently as he explained

She didn't completely understand the words he said but she understood enough

The world held its breath as it waited for Mary's answer

God waited

Gabriel waited

What if she said no?

Mary didn't say no, she said yes.

She believed Gabriel

She believed God's Word

She trusted Him completely.

She knew what He asked of her wouldn't be easy

Mary knew that but she still said yes

From that moment she put her whole life in God's Hands

When Mary replied yes the world's salvation was conceived.

She carried the Saviour of the world in her womb.

His name was Joseph

He was also from the town of Nazareth

He was a carpenter and he was engaged to Mary

He loved her with all his heart.

When he learned that she was with Child he was very upset

He was confused and angry

How could she do this to him?

How could she betray him with another man?

Joseph had a dream

In his dream an Angel of God came to him

Joseph believed the Angel

He believed in God's Word

He trusted God

He and Mary got married.

Joseph and Mary made the long and dangerous journey to Bethlehem

Mary was heavy with Child

The inns were all full that night due to the census

It was in a stable that the Holy Son of God was born.

The donkey, the cattle and the lambs were the first creatures to see their Creator in the flesh.

Blessed be God!

Blessed be Jesus!

Blessed be His Mother Mary!

Blessed be His foster-father Joseph!

God is indeed with His people.

Many years passed

Jesus was now thirty years old

It was time for Him to begin His Work

He chose His disciples one by one

He walked with them

He taught them the Way, the Truth and the Life.

He invited people to change their way of thinking

He invited people to change their attitude toward the marginalized of the community

Some people listened to Him

The majority of people ignored Him.

One of His friends betrayed Jesus

Yes, one of His chosen turned his back on the Saviour

The soldiers beat Jesus

They cruelly tortured Jesus

They put a crown of thorns upon His Head

They nailed Him to a Cross

It is the Cross of our salvation.

Such Love for His people!

Such obedience to His Father!

Such perfect unconditional Love Jesus had for His Father

Such perfect obedience regardless of the cost

Before Jesus took His last agonizing breath He showed Mercy to His accusers

He forgave them

He forgave the men who had tortured Him

He forgave the men who had scourged Him

He forgave the men who had hammered the nails into His Hands and His Feet

He forgave them!

Such love Jesus has for us

He shed His precious Blood to wash away our sins

Not just my sins

Not just your sins

He shed His Precious Blood to wash away the sins of the whole world

Such absolute Love!

On the third day God the Father showed how much He loved His Son

He resurrected Jesus from the grave

The disciples were frightened

They were downright terrified

They had lost their friend, their leader and their teacher
They didn't know what to do so they hid.
The risen Jesus appeared to His disciples
He didn't criticize them for their lack of faith
He gave them His Peace
He promised to send the Holy Spirit to them
Then Jesus was gone
He had returned to His Father in Heaven.
Come, Holy Spirit, come!
The Holy Spirit came to the disciples
He came as tongues of fire
He gave them strength and He gave them courage
With conviction and faith they spread the Good News of Jesus
With conviction and faith they told the world about Jesus.

MY MUSE

I have a sheet of paper in front of me
It's white
It's still blank
I have a pen in my hand
I'm ready to write
Patiently I wait
I wait for the words to come.
I call to my muse
She doesn't answer
It seems that she's not ready
It seems that she's asleep.
Half an hour passes
The sheet of paper is still empty
It's still blank
No ink marks cover it
Writer's block
Is that what I've got?
I put the pen and the paper aside
I take Odin for his evening walk
I go to bed.
My muse wakes me up
It's the middle of the night
Now she's wide awake
Now she's raring to go
Now is the time to write.

CLOUDS

From my balcony I watched the clouds
They were racing across the sky
They weren't soft, white and fluffy
They were dark and ominous
They were getting ready for a wild party
There was definitely a storm on the way.
The storm was short lived but violent
The wind howled
Bending tree branches kissed the ground
The rain came down in torrents
It soaked the earth
The thunder rumbled loudly overhead
The light show was spectacular.

EMOTIONS

I glared at him, my husband of twenty years
I loved him
At this moment though anger flashed from my green eyes
"Don't do this to me," I cried
"You told me yesterday that you would come with me
Now you tell me that you're sorry
Now you tell me that you can't come
I want to know why
I want you to tell me."
"I don't feel at all well," he replied
"My head is pounding
I think someone is using it as a drum
I just wouldn't be good company tonight."
I knew that he was telling the truth
I knew about his headaches
I knew the pain he suffered when he had one
My anger slowly evaporated
An expression of disappointment crossed my face
I understood though
What an inopportune time for a headache to come knocking
Why did it have to come on the same evening as this important family celebration?
Darn it!
I had to attend it, I had to be there
I kissed my husband gently
I promised not to be late.
When I arrived home just after eleven
He was in bed asleep

I knew that's where he would be
It was actually the best place for him.
I undressed in the darkness
I crawled into bed and snuggled beside him
Odin barked softly then all was quiet.

WHAT IS LIFE? (1)

What is life?

That's a loaded question

Sometimes life is a challenge, sometimes life is an adventure

At times life is just a plain drag.

I know one thing for sure

Life is a gift from God

It's an on-going process

Every experience I have, every person I meet, influences me in some way

It teaches me something

It makes me laugh or cry or grow.

To accept myself as I am with all my faults and weaknesses makes it much easier for me to accept others as they are.

To anticipate a future plan is half the fun of getting there.

To be aware of God's presence in the people around me is sometimes difficult.

To care for myself and others isn't easy without love.

To carry my burdens and complain makes me think of Jesus carrying His Cross in silence.

To celebrate special occasions with family and friends renews my spirit.

To cry tears of joy or tears of sorrow is a good emotional release.

To dance is fun and good exercise.

To die to my bad habits one at a time is a good New Year's resolution.

To enjoy nature is very relaxing.

To explore new ideas and new places fills my mind with knowledge.

To finish a project fills me with joy.

To forgive myself for hurting others by words or actions sets me free.

To frown when things go wrong only makes matters worse.

To gaze at the night sky fills me with awe.

To help prevent extinction of wildlife and its habitat is a good cause.

To help someone by a simple act of kindness lightens his or her burden.

To have faith in the Blessed Trinity gives me strength.

To joke about other cultures is not amusing.

To laugh helps me when I feel down.

To learn something new every day keeps my mind active.

To let go of old grudges relieves stress.

To love and to be loved in return is a treasure worth more than gold.

To motivate myself to be more than a couch potato is sometimes a real challenge.

To participate in community activities helps me to get to know my neighbours.

To pray for peace is one of my daily rituals.

To read a good book is very enjoyable for me.

To sleep in my husband's arms still thrills me even after twenty-five years of marriage.

To smile at another person lights up his or her day.

To talk nonsense or to talk serious issues is important between spouses.

To venture into the unknown takes courage.

To wait for a bus teaches me patience.

To walk is the most natural exercise there is.

To wonder when humans will live together in peace is a thought that often flows through my mind.

To write poetry and short stories fills me with delight.

To die is just another dimension of life.

THE DREAM(1)

Last night I had a dream
It was a very strange dream
I dreamt that I was riding a unicorn
Why I was riding a unicorn instead of a horse I don't know.
The unicorn was sure of foot and swift in speed
Where we were going in such a hurry I don't know.
We went through a grassy meadow
We went over a wooden bridge
The unicorn began to climb a hill
The hill became steeper with each step he took.
Suddenly he stopped and shook his mane
I looked around and almost fell off
There was a cloud right beside me
I lowered my gaze
I saw the earth far below me
What were we doing up here in the sky?
I don't know.

WHO I AM

I am an alpha

A foetus in my mother's womb then a baby at her breast

I am a sister, a daughter, a cousin and a friend.

A child starting kindergarten

A teenager graduating from Grade 8

A young woman in high school

A college graduate seeking her first job and her first apartment

I am a twenty-four year old woman in love

Now I'm a woman with a broken heart.

I am a woman seeking better employment

An aunt to my nieces and nephews

I am a mid-thirty woman in love again

Now I am a wife, a confidant, a lover and a friend.

A woman who was downsized

A woman who does volunteer work

A dog owner

I am a woman who loves to read, to travel and to learn.

A woman who loves to spend quiet evenings at home with my husband

A woman who is growing older

I am a woman who still has lots to give

A woman who still has lots of living to do!

IT'S STILL YOU (1)

My husband, this poem is for you
You make me laugh and you make me cry
You make me smile with love.
Your arms hold me through the long night
Your smile greets me at dawn's first light
Your voice sounds like music to my ears
Your face delights me whenever you are near.
You tiptoe into my dreams
You hold my heart in your hands
You have made my life complete
Your know it's true
It's still you!
You're my husband, you're my love, and you're my man.
It's still you after all these years
It will still be you a hundred years from now
It will always be you, my husband.

MY PRAYER

Lord Jesus, I thank You for this brand new day

I know that You will show me the way

I pray for my family, my relatives and my friends

Thank You for the love we share

Keep us in Your tender care

For peace in the world I do pray

I believe there will be peace some day

I say a prayer for all the sick, the lonely and the homeless

Let me do whatever I can to being a little joy into their lives.

I pray for all the people who have died

Members of my family

The people killed in acts of war, terrorism, violence and natural disasters

Their souls have gone to the hereafter

They rest now in Your Peace, Lord Jesus

They rest in Your Light

They rest in Your Love for all eternity.

PART THREE

NATURE'S HEALING

The whispering breeze softly touches my hair

The winding roads I walk with care

The singing birds soothe my soul

The rainbow above makes me feel whole.

The ringing laughter echoes through the night

The flowers open their eyes with the day's new light

I remain in the ancient cave until the very end

The passing hours are more precious now my true friend.

MOTHER EARTH

Mother Earth, I feel your pain

The humans of my time are destroying you

You once had clean, clear, pure water in your lakes

In your rivers and oceans and seas too

Now most of them are polluted with nuclear waste and other human-made garbage

The birds that eat the fish die from this poison.

When the water is all gone

When it is no longer fit for human or animal consumption what then?

Humans know that water is necessary for all survival

Do only a few of us care?

I hear the trees crying when they are cut down

The humans from the big lumber companies don't see the damage they are doing

They only see dollar signs in front of their eyes

When the trees are all gone what then?

I grieve for all the animals that have become extinct

Humans have invaded their habitat, their territory, in the name of progress

Do we really need more industrial parks, more shopping malls and more condominiums?

Poachers have killed wild animals for their ivory or for their organs

Wild, majestic animals have gone forever for human need

It's more like human greed.

When the wild animals are all gone what then?

Will we be sorry for what we've done?

Will we miss the howl of the wolf?

The roar of the mighty jungle beasts

The thundering of caribou hooves

Will humans finally cry in utter despair?

We have treated our wild companions badly.

Mother Earth, humans are polluting your air

We are polluting your precious air with chemicals whose names I can't even pronounce

Pollution in your atmosphere has caused the hole in the Ozone layer to grow larger

It has caused drastic changes in the weather patterns.

You are rebelling with severe droughts, floods and hurricanes

There's no telling what Nature will do next

The havoc you dealt to Florida, the Bahamas. Jamaica and especially New Orleans

The destruction left behind by the wind and the water is just a warning to us

Smarten up or things will get worse.

Humans have ravaged you, Mother Earth

Rusting tanks and other weapons of mass destruction mar the beauty of various countries

Land mines lie hidden in the ground waiting to injure you

They will injure us too but unfortunately we don't seem to care

Exploding bombs have left gaping holes in your landscape.

Mother Earth, humans of my time haven't respected your gifts

They have abused you

They have treated you with disdain

You aren't going to let us get away with it

I hear you moaning in pain

You will take your revenge in your own good time

The cruelty, the greed and the absolute stupidity of humankind horrifies you

You follow the laws of God; we seem to follow our own laws

We follow whatever law suits us at the time

You have given us several warnings, Mother Earth, but we don't seem to listen.

Mother Earth, is there any way that humans can make it up to you?

You remain silent then suddenly you shudder in agony

Another falling tree shakes the ground

Another elephant is slaughtered for his ivory

Then you answer

You send a tornado sweeping through the American mid-west.

Will we ever care about the consequences of our actions?

Will we ever learn?

Is there any hope for us at all?

STOP!

Stop!

Stop cutting down the rainforest

The panda bear and the other wildlife that live there are suffering

We are destroying their habitat

Do we not care?

Once they are gone they are gone forever.

Stop!

Stop polluting the air

We have to breathe it

The poisons that we spew into the air are making us sick

They are killing us and all the species who share the earth with us.

Stop!

Stop polluting the water

We have to drink it

The chemicals that farmers spread on their fields

The nuclear waste from large factories

This all seeps into the streams, the lakes, the rivers and the oceans

It kills the fish and the water birds

It goes into our drinking water causing sickness and even death.

Stop!

Stop killing the wild animals

The magnificent tiger, the sleek wolf, the thunderous elephant have a right to live.

Stop!

Stop flooding the land with their blood

Stop using their fur for rugs and their body parts for trinkets and even medicine.

Stop!

Stop killing each other with harsh words and lies

Stop using loud voices and fists

Stop killing each other with guns, knives and bombs.

Stop!

Stop the assault on Mother Earth.

Stop!

Stop the assault on animals.

Stop!

Stop the assault on humans whose skin colour or culture or lifestyle is different from ours.

Stop!

Please stop before the earth and her gifts are completely ruined

Please stop before there's nothing and nobody left

Please stop before it's too late.

Stop!

Please stop before we all become extinct.

THE VOWS

I remember the day we wed
I remember the vows we said
We took each other as husband and wife
We gave each other our thoughts and our hearts
We gave each other our love and our lives.
We vowed to have, to hold, to love and to cherish each other forever
We pledged our love before God and our guests
We pledged to be faithful to each other
It didn't matter if the times were good or bad
It didn't matter if the times were joyful or sad
We pledged each other our hearts until the day death would us part.
We have stayed together through sunny and stormy weather
Through thick and thin we have stayed together
Through times of despair and times of wonder
We've been there for each other just as we promised.

TO THE MAN I LOVE

You are my husband, my lover and my confidant
You are my best friend too
No matter where we go
No matter what we do
You know that we will never part
You will always be in my thoughts and in my prayers
You will stay forever in my heart.

LOVE`S SONG (1)

Love`s song is a warm embrace
Love`s song is a smiling face
Love`s song is a guiding light
It shines through the darkest night.
Love`s song is a faithful friend
She`s always waiting around the bend
Love`s song is music so sweet
Love`s song is the tear we weep.
Love`s song is a whispered word
Love`s song is always heard
Love`s song is a flowing stream
Love`s song is a waking dream.
Love`s song is doing what`s right
Love`s song is a star so bright
Love`s song is a quiet space
Love`s song is a sacred place.
Love`s song is one of courage
Its music is different on every page
Love`s song is together growing old
Love`s song is much more than a band of gold.
Love`s song is showing that we care
Love`s song is carrying the pain we share
Love`s song always understands you
Love`s song is forever true.
Love`s song grows deep within
It`s music can be loud or dim
Love`s song is here to stay
Love`s song will never fade away.

MISSING YOU

I ran up the stairs and down the hall
I unlocked the apartment door
I prayed that you would still be there
I had to see your face once more.
You were sitting in your favourite chair
You stood up and held me tight
You said that you had missed me too
Let's give our love another chance
Why don't we begin tonight?

FOR MY SISTER

We don't see each other very often
We have such different personalities
Our lives are full of so many different things
When we do get together for lunch
The time spent with you goes by much too fast
We each have our trials and tribulations
We each have our happy times too
For all that you've done and for all that you do
For just being you
I wish you only the best
I want you to know I'm proud to have a sister like you.

FOR MY BROTHER

This poem is just for you
It`s sent across the miles
We live such different lives
We have each accomplished our goals one at a time
We have each endured many experiences
Some of them were life-changing
Others were very pleasant and happy
A few were not but they are part of us too
Though we rarely see each other I think of you often
I send you best wishes across the miles.

CHRISTMAS(1)

A new time is coming

A new day is dawning

Will you be ready for Christmas morn when the Saviour of the world
was born?

Christmas is more than gifts under the tree

It's more than wine, turkey, Christmas pudding and mincemeat pie

It's more than love between you and me

It's more than being with friends and family.

Christmas is the Birthday of God's only Son

Some people want to remove Christ from Christmas

I don't think it can be done.

Christmas is more than a holiday

It's more than just a day of fun

Christmas is a Holy Day of celebration and thanksgiving

It's the day when God gave his Son to the world

Jesus will show human beings a new way of living

He will show us a new way of giving.

This is the time to know the true meaning of Christmas

This is the place right here and right now

Will you make the time?

Are you awake?

Will I make the time?

Are you ready to give birth to Christ in your heart?

Are you ready to let Him reign there forever?

Are you ready to let Him bring you peace?

Am I?

THE CHRISTMAS MESSAGE

The Christmas message is one of peace

It is one of love, it is one of hope

It is a gift from God above.

The Christmas message is one of beauty

It is one of joy, it is one of giving

It is from Mary's little boy.

The Christmas message is one to be followed

It is one to be received and understood

It is one to be believed.

Why can't humans live together in peace?

Why do we hurt each other with cruel words?

Why do we continue to kill each other with dangerous weapons?

Why do thousands of men and women and children die violent deaths?

Deaths caused by terrorism and war

Why can't humans live together in peace?

The Christmas message is one of peace

The Angels sang about it on that first Christmas day

Even if we continue to ignore it the Christmas message is here to stay.

WHAT I WANT FOR CHRISTMAS

What do I want for Christmas?
I`ll tell you if I may
I would like world peace
That`s what I`d like on the Lord`s Birthday.
When, oh when, will the rivers of blood stop flowing?
When, oh when, will the circles of love start growing?
When, oh when, will human blood stop soaking into the sand?
When, oh, when, will there be peace in that beautiful land?
When, oh when, will man`s inhumanity to man stop?
When, oh when, will we finally grow up?
When, oh when, will the greed and the evil be gone?
When, oh when, will the right finally overcome the wrong?
When, oh when, will humankind finally understand?
I would really like to know the answer
Tell me, friend, if you can.

HALLOWEEN

It's Halloween night

It's time for little children to dress up

A goblin arrives at my door

Here comes a ghost and a witch

Now it's a cowboy and a princess

It's an angel and a bunny rabbit

There's a little slugger and an astronaut

Oh my goodness, it's Superman and a kitten.

I give them an apple or a chocolate bar

Maybe a box of raisins or a package of gum

There's pennies for UNICEF for everyone.

It's nine-thirty and the evening's done

I make a cup of tea and sit on the sofa

I reminisce about the years long since gone when my mother took me trick or treating.

THANKSGIVING DAY

On this Thanksgiving Day 2004
What am I really thankful for?
My health both mental and physical
My family and friends and my husband too
The love we share is lasting and true.
The companionship of Odin, my dog
When I'm feeling down
He's such a good buddy to have around
My country, Canada
Such a beautiful place to live
Thank You, dear God, for everything You give.

PENTECOST

Holy Spirit of God, come down!

Take away our human greed

Fill us instead with the seed of Your Love.

Holy Spirit, descend!

Descend into the darkness of this world

Both within and without there is sin

Fill the world and us with Your blessed Light.

Holy Spirit of God, come down!

Give humans the wisdom to make all wars cease

Fly into our lives, O Dove

Help us to make this earth a place of peace.

Holy Spirit of God, come down!

Take away our human selfishness

Give us the courage to do what's right

No matter how difficult it may be

Help us to see with our hearts and not just our eyes.

Holy Spirit of God, we need you!

Come down and help us, please

Fill our minds with the right kind of knowledge

Help us to treat each other with respect

Help us to make this world a better place

For all the creatures who live here.

Holy Spirit of God, descend!

Descend into the hurry and the worry of our busy world

Come into our hearts

Give us patience that we may stop and see and understand God's wonderful gifts to us

Holy Spirit of God

Come down from Heaven we pray
We sigh for You today
The day of Pentecost!

WORRY

When I worry it doesn't change anything
It doesn't do any good at all
Worrying is a waste of mental energy
Energy that I could use in a more positive way
I want to break this bad habit of worrying
I will succeed one day.
The next time I begin to worry I'll say a prayer instead
I'll refuse to let any negative thoughts enter into my head
I'll put the worry into God's Hands
I'll put it in His Care.

NOTHINGNESS(1)

The snow fell on my uncovered head

The wind burned my bare hands

I walked then I ran

I had no idea where I was going

I didn't care

I just had to get away from that place.

The city streets were far behind me now

It was almost dark

The snow still fell in silent, gentle flakes.

My legs grew weary

My breath came in gasps

I tripped and fell into a dark emptiness

My body seemed to dissolve into nothingness

Soon the snow covered me like a blanket.

My mind forgot that mangled body

It was the remains of a human being I had known and loved.

For a long time I was hot and then cold

Sweats were followed by shivers

Feverish images occupied my brain

Strange voices haunted my thoughts.

I don't remember how long I was delirious

It could have been hours or even days

There were people nearby talking but the words they said made no
sense to me,

Eventually the fever broke

I woke up

I lay in my own bed weak and exhausted.

My husband held a cup to my lips

The liquid I drank was hot and slightly sweet.
Sleep now enveloped me like a soft cloud
No disquieting dreams this time just peaceful sleep.

FROM ONE MINUTE TO THE NEXT: ANTHOLOGY OF AN ACCIDENT

In the blink of an eye our Christmas plans changed

My husband, Keith, our dog, Odin and me had driven from Toronto
to Peterborough

We were going to spend the holidays with my parents

We avoided the huge snowstorm that hit Toronto by leaving a day earlier
than usual

Safe and sound at the Quality Inn we were.

Who knows what will happen from one minute to the next?

Keith walked down the hall to the breakfast room to get two plates

We were going to share some Christmas cake.

I heard a crash, a scream, and then an urgent knock on the door

A woman stood there.

"Your husband's fallen and hurt himself," she said.

I grabbed the key and followed her

I almost lost my head when I saw the amount of blood on the carpet.

Keith had lost his balance and tripped

The plates went flying and broke

He landed on a piece of glass

His left arm and hand were very badly cut.

The manager had already phoned for the ambulance

God bless her!

I ran back to the room and put on my coat and my hat

Quickly, I grabbed my husband's coat from the hanger

I patted Odin and told him to be a good boy

He whined softly, he knew that something wasn't right.

I put the "Do Not Disturb" sign on the door and retraced my steps
down the hall.

The paramedics had just arrived

I went with Keith to the Peterborough Hospital

He went to emergency and I went to the waiting room.

Two-and-a-half hours passed before I was allowed to see him

He had fifteen stitches in his left arm and three stitches in the thumb of his left hand.

The doctor informed me that he'd have to be transferred to St. Michael's Hospital in Toronto.

Why?

He had damaged the nerves of three fingers on his left hand

He would need plastic surgery done.

I sighed deeply.

So Keith went to Toronto and I returned to the Quality Inn.

It's now eight o'clock in the morning of Christmas Eve

My dear husband is supposed to be operated on in one hour.

I said a prayer for him and waited

I was still waiting at two-thirty in the afternoon.

I phoned St. Michael's Hospital only to receive the news that Keith's operation had been delayed

A trauma case had come in

I hung up the phone and took a deep breath

I would have to be patient.

A few minutes later the phone rang – it was my mother

"There's a ray of sunshine to light up this stressful day," she said.

You remember the snowstorm I mentioned earlier

My sister and brother-in-law's flight to Calgary had been cancelled.

After a brief conversation with my sister I breathed a little easier

God bless her and her husband!

Neither will believe it but I do believe that they are angels in disguise.

You ask why I'm not in Toronto with my husband

You ask why I remained in Peterborough

Those are fair questions!

I'm not a hard-hearted wife

I knew my sweetheart was in good hands

He was being well looked after and he would want me to visit with my parents on Christmas Day

The minutes ticked by one at a time

So slowly they passed.

I phoned St. Michael's Hospital twice more during the day

I was told that Keith was still waiting.

My sister phoned me at ten-thirty on Christmas Eve with the news I'd been waiting for:

He's had his operation and is in the recovery room.

Thank You, Lord Jesus!

I phoned my parents and passed on the good news

"Thanks be to God," they said

"Amen!" I replied.

When I phoned the hospital on Christmas morning I had a feeling that my husband wouldn't be released any time soon.

He was in pain

I said a prayer for him.

Odin and I drove to my parent's house where we tried to celebrate Christmas

We ate a nice meal

My mother had even made a few treats for Odin.

We opened our gifts but our hearts weren't really in it

Someone we loved was missing.

The dog and I returned to Toronto a few days later

When I visited Keith in the hospital a nurse was with him

I smiled when she told me that he could go home

When?

"Today!" she replied.

I went to admitting to retrieve his valuables

Everything was there except for his eyeglasses.

Where were his eyeglasses?

I inquired at the nurse's station

A nurse phoned the emergency department where Keith had arrived five days earlier

A thorough check of the area was made but no eyeglasses were found.

He couldn't go home without his glasses!

Does Keith have a locker?

Of course.

I saw his winter coat and hat

I saw a plastic bag which contained his slacks, shirt, socks and underwear too

What was in the smaller plastic bag?

His shoes!

You will never believe in a month of Sundays where I found his glasses!

In his left shoe!

I'm telling you, it's true!

Discharge procedures were followed

The release papers were signed and at four-ten the taxi pulled up at our apartment building.

A few minutes later I unlocked our door

Odin was overjoyed to see us both.

He sniffed at my husband's hand then looked up at him and whined as if to say:

"Welcome home!"

I echoed the sentiment.

WORDS

Black words on paper
White spaces between
What do the words say?
What do they mean!
There are words about politics, words about faith
There are words about sports, words about hate.
There are words that hurt and words that heal
Words that make me laugh and words that make me ill.
Words spoken by the human voice go out into the air
They can be foul or they can be fair.
Once the words are spoken they can never be taken back
If humans remember anything they should remember that!

MY QUEST

I ran out the door onto the porch to see my new bicycle

I wanted to ride it again

Only it wasn't there: it was gone

It had been stolen.

I had bought it only yesterday on my tenth birthday

I had saved my allowance, my birthday money and my Christmas money since I was seven

I was broken-hearted and I cried.

It's now my twenty-first birthday

I've saved money from summer jobs since I was seventeen

Saved money from the job I've had for three years as a carpenter.

Finally I had enough money to buy the car of my dreams.

It was a Ford Mustang painted fire engine red

Less than a month later it was gone.

It had been stolen.

I reported it to the police

A week later they found the remains

It had been stripped inside and out

I was angry and I was upset

I wondered what to do now.

I walked to the bicycle shop and chose one I liked

It was a Raleigh and it was painted earth green.

BLACK ICE

It took less than a second.

In the blink of an eye the wheels of the car I was driving it a patch of black ice

The car skidded and hit something

I don't remember what.

My life flashed before me:

The things I'd done or not done

The words I'd spoken or the words not spoken

The people I'd helped or the ones I'd hurt.

Then I saw a Light

It was the most brilliant, the most beautiful Light I'd ever seen.

A Voice spoke from the Light

"Go back," It said

I didn't want to go back

I wanted to stay

The minutes passed and still I lingered

Still I hesitated

I wanted to stay but I knew I couldn't

Something told me that it wasn't yet my time

The Voice insisted

I obeyed and returned to my body.

DEPRESSION

Life is strange, life is funny
One day everything is going fine
I'm way up on cloud nine.
The next day I'm lost
I'm lost in my pain
I'm lost in the depths of my depression.
It takes a long time to come out of it.
Days turn into weeks and weeks into months
Then one sunny day I begin to see the light
The light shines at the end of a long dark tunnel.
It's a wonderful moment
I know, yes, now I know
I know that I'm going to be all right.

SIMPLE PLEASURES*

Arranging flowers in a vase
Reading a good book
Holding hands with my husband
Playing with my dog
These are the simple pleasures I cherish.
Having lunch with my sister
Watching a butterfly land on a leaf
Visiting a friend in need
These are the things I treasure.

TODAY

A noise invades the silence of my dream
It's Odin whining to go out
I open my eyes and glance at the red numbers on the clock radio
It's just after five-thirty
Might as well get up
My husband has a doctor's appointment this morning.
I get dressed and take Odin for a walk
I breathe in the cool, snow-laden air
We return to find my husband up
He's making coffee.
Thank you!
After he leaves, I do the laundry and sweep the floor
Then I wash my hair
I check the email on the computer
Most of it is spam
I read my new novel for half an hour or so
Prepare a bag of clothes for the Salvation Army.
Odin and I walk to the bank
There are always bills to be paid
We stop at the Post Office to mail some letters
I brush the dog when we get home.
Time for a coffee – that's better!
The phone rings – it's Keith
He's finished his doctor's appointment
Do I want to meet him for lunch?
Good idea, said I
For dessert I have apple pie.
We pick up the dry cleaning and go to the drug store

We walk home together in the snow.

I hope there are no more chores to do but there are

I take the recycle bag down to the big blue box

I get the mail and guess what?

Odin has to go out again.

The three of us take a little nap

Oh goodness, it's time to start dinner.

It's been a busy day

I think we'll order from Swiss Chalet.

I feed Odin and take him for his evening walk

We watch the news and then CSI

I have a nice hot bath and then to bed, to sleep

Maybe Odin won't wake me up so early tomorrow.

*IT SHOULDN'T MATTER
BUT IT DOES* (1)

It shouldn't matter if my skin is white or black or red

It shouldn't matter if I sleep on the street or in a comfortable bed

It shouldn't matter if I wear a turban or a woollen hat on my hair

It shouldn't matter if I am mentally or physically challenged or never have a care

It shouldn't matter if I live on welfare or go to a job each day

It shouldn't matter if I'm young or old or if I've lost my way

It shouldn't matter if I live in a house or in a cardboard box on the street

It shouldn't matter if I have a friend or nobody at all to meet

It shouldn't matter if I'm a genius or have little education

It shouldn't matter if I'm a carpenter or the president of a nation

It shouldn't matter if I'm fat or slim or if I have children or not

It shouldn't matter if I live in a country that's cold or a country that's hot

It shouldn't matter if I wear hand-me-downs or buy my clothes brand new

It shouldn't matter if I'm a chatterbox or never express my point of view.

It shouldn't matter but it does

I really don't know why

It shouldn't matter but it does

It makes me want to cry.

It shouldn't matter because we are all human beings

We should treat each other with respect

We should treat each other with gratitude and appreciation

We are all children of God

Don't you know that yet?

Yes, every single one of us is a child of God
We are all children of God
It doesn't matter what name we give Him
It doesn't matter our colour, our race or our creed
Each one of us one day should see God's Face.

AT TIMES LIKE THESE

Sometimes I wake up so confused
I feel like I'm living in a daze
Sometimes I feel so very afraid
It's like I'm walking through a maze.
Sometimes my husband gets severe headaches
They make him feel so down
He goes to bed and stays there all day
I worry so much that I'm bowed to the ground.
At times like these it's difficult to feel the Lord's presence
Yet somehow we know He's near
He holds us close
He holds us so gently
He tells us that there's nothing to fear.

RUMOUR'S WORDS HURT

I don't remember the colour of your hair
I don't remember the clothes you wore
I just remember the words that you said
Words that cut me to the core
The words you said were not true
I don't know how you could tell such lies about me.
Your words made me feel like a nobody
Lower than a worm is how they made me feel
I want to tell you something
I know the feeling well.
I remember when I said words about a co-worker
The words were not true
She asked me how I could say such a thing
I didn't know how to answer her question.
I apologized but she turned away
She felt sad
I felt ashamed
This may sound strange to you
I want to thank you for teaching me a lesson
I thought I'd already learned this lesson
Obviously I hadn't
Words from a rumour shouldn't be repeated
They hurt.
Words from a rumour should stop with you and me.

THE MAN FROM POLAND

Several years ago a little boy was born in Poland
The child was destined for greatness
He saw many changes during his lifetime
He influenced many minds
He touched numerous hearts with his love and kindness
He was ordained a priest
Years later he was elected as Pope.
Karol Wojtyla took the name of Pope John Paul II.
He was a man of prayer and a man of courage
He was a man of humility and a man of patience
He was a man of spirituality and a man of understanding
He was a man of action and a man of faith
During years of trials and illness he never once lost his faith in God.

ARE WE LEARNING YET?

A long time ago when God created the earth

He made more than enough of everything

For all the human beings there would ever be

That is, if each person would take his or her share and no more

Something got in the way

Something called greed.

Now the gap between rich and poor is no longer a gap

It has become a gulf.

Will we ever be able to build a bridge to cross over?

Many of our brothers and sisters are in need

They don't even have the basic necessities of life

They don't have clean water, shelter, food or medicine.

Will we ever learn to share?

How many more children will go to bed hungry?

How many more men, women and children will die of HIV/Aids and other diseases due to lack of the proper medicine?

How many more children will die of malnutrition?

The big drug companies have the medicine

Unfortunately they are more interested in making a profit

If the poor people can't pay then they don't get the necessary medicine

To me that is just wrong.

How many more human beings will die before we learn to care?

All of us need to learn to care

Not just a few of us but all of us

I mean every person on this planet

We have to learn to share the bounteousness of our earth with one another.

When, oh when will greed take flight?
When, oh when will we let love rule the earth?
When, oh when will we get it right?

BUNDLE WEEKEND

This pair of slacks doesn't fit me anymore

Maybe that's an incentive to lose a pound or four

This blouse I bought two years ago

I've never worn it

Perhaps someone else could use it.

I liked this purse when I bought it but now I don't

It goes into the bag for St. Vincent de Paul.

This jacket is slightly worn but it's still okay

Look at this pair of shoes

Why on earth did I buy them?

Goodbye, shoes.

There's another blouse, hardly used

This purse can definitely go.

In the linen closet I find a set of sheets and a blanket to be added.

The kitchen yields two saucepans and some plates I don't need.

Why not let someone else have them?

What's this?

A teddy bear that will make a child happy

Here's another teddy bear to add.

I go through the clothes cupboard again and find a few more items

A sweater, another pair of slacks, a few of my husband's shirts

And this!

A backpack to put everything in

I walk down the street to the church

The St. Vincent de Paul truck is parked in the lot

I deposit my offerings then watch while several other people to the same.

FALLEN HEROES

Four black horses riderless now
Four young mounted policemen ambushed
Shot down in the line of duty
In the prime of their lives
Grieving family and friends water the earth with their tears
Wondering how such a thing could happen
Knowing that in the coming years
The pain in their aching hearts will be eased
Hoping that their questions will somehow be answered
They send their prayers to God above
Knowing that the souls of their loved ones are with Him

I SEE YOU (1)

I see you

Do I really see you?

Do I really see you with all your pain, your joy, your dreams and your hopes?

Is it really you I see or do I just see another person taking up space on this earth?

A stranger that maybe I want to know or maybe I don't

Are you just another person getting in the way of my life?

If I saw you as you are

If I saw you with all your worry, your loneliness and your frustration who would I really see?

If I looked into your eyes instead of looking at the ground

Maybe my life would be better

I'll never know until I take the time to see you as you really are.

MY CITY FILLED

My city is filled with buildings

Factories, offices, condominiums and houses

Asphalt roads and thousands of cars take up the green spaces

The parks are reduced to almost nothing.

Where will the children play?

Where will the dogs run?

My city is filled with heat, smog and humidity

Everyone is wilting

People gather anywhere that has air conditioning

The coffee shops, the bookstores

Even the churches are filled to overflowing

Everyone wants to breathe cool air.

When will it rain and wipe away the dust and the sweat of my city?

My city is filled with danger

There are killings on the streets

Groups of teenagers shed one another's blood

They have so little pity.

When will they learn that violence is not the answer to their problems?

My city is filled with people

People from dozens of different countries and cultures

Music and dance and noise are everywhere

Young and old

Strangers, friends and lovers will meet at their special place

They will meet at their private space somewhere in the city

Somewhere in the city we all call home.

GOD LIVES (1)

God lives in the clouds
In every drop of rain
He lives in every bird that flies
He's even in our pain.
God lives in the falling snow
In every beautiful flower
He lives in every shining star
He's with us every hour.
God lives in the warm sunshine
In every blade of grass
He wants to live within our hearts
All we need to do is ask.
God lives in every loving touch
In every peaceful night
He's in every butterfly
He's in every dawn's first light.
God lives in the wind that blows
In every longing sigh
He's in every smile we give
In every newborn baby's cry
God lives in all of His creation
In every gift we share
He's in every mountain and stream
God is everywhere!

SOUNDS – A LIFE SPENT

While walking in the park one day
A man heard a loud noise
It almost sounded like a car backfiring but it wasn't
It was the sound of gunfire.
What a silly person, he thought
He heard the noise a second time
Could it be the sniper he had heard about on the radio that morning?
The thought crossed his mind that he should head for home
He headed in that direction
He hadn't walked very far when a bullet hit him in the chest
Slowly he fell
He felt the soft grass beneath him.
He saw flashbacks of his life
He heard sounds in his head.
A dog barked.
A horse neighed.
A baby cried.
A woman laughed.
A man moaned in pain.
Drops of rain hit the window.
Wine glasses clicked.
The telephone rang.
A train whistle blew.
Waves lapped against the shore.
A car engine roared.
A book dropped on the floor.
Computer keys clicked.
Loud voices shouted in anger.

A door slammed.

Footsteps walked down the stairs.

Bagpipes played.

Sirens wailed.

The man listened to his own laboured breathing

He felt hands on his body

He heard a voice whisper urgent words and replied

 "God, I am truly sorry for all my sins."

He felt cold, so very cold

His life force was slowly ebbing away

His blood flowed onto the grass.

He heard a soft voice whisper his name

Felt her tears on his face

He gasped briefly trying desperately to get air

He couldn't manage

It was just too much effort.

He closed his eyes and thought he heard an Angel singing.

WHAT IS LIFE (2)

What is life?

That's a million dollar question

Sometimes life is an adventure, sometimes life is a challenge and sometimes life is just a plain drag.

I believe that life is an on-going process

Every experience I have, every person I meet teaches me something.

Like what?

Well, accepting myself as I am with all my faults and weaknesses makes it much easier for me to accept others as they are.

Being aware of God's love in the people around me is sometimes difficult.

Believing in the Blessed Trinity – God the Father, God the Son and God the Holy Spirit – gives me strength.

Breaking my bad habits one at a time is always a good New Year's resolution.

Caring for myself and others is easy when I do it with love.

Celebrating special occasions with family and friends renews my spirit.

Crying tears of joy or tears of sorrow is a good emotional release.

Enjoying nature – the whispering breeze, the fragrance of flowers, the serenade of songbirds – is always relaxing.

Exploring new ideas and new places fills my mind with knowledge.

Forgiving myself for things I've said or done that has hurt others and asking forgiveness of the people I have hurt sets me free.

Frowning when things go wrong only makes matters worse.

Gazing at the night sky fills me with wonder.

Helping to prevent extinction of wildlife and its habitat is something I like to do.

Ignoring personal problems until they become overwhelming is not a good idea.

Joking about other cultures is not amusing.

Knitting is a good way to relax.

Knowing something is wrong and doing it anyway could have serious consequences.

Laughing helps me when I feel down.

Learning something new every day keeps my mind active.

Loving and being loved in return is a treasure worth more than gold.

Meeting an old friend unexpectedly is always a wonderful pleasure.

Motivating myself to be more than a couch potato is sometimes a real challenge.

Napping for half an hour in the afternoon revitalizes me.

Owning a dog is a pleasure as well as a responsibility.

Participating in community activities helps me to get to know my neighbours.

Praying for peace is one of my daily rituals.

Reading is a very enjoyable activity for me.

Remembering the veterans who served our country is a way of thanking them for the sacrifices they made.

Sleeping in my husband's arms still thrills me even after twenty-three years of marriage.

Starting over is very difficult but sometimes it's necessary.

Talking nonsense or talking serious issues my husband and I always keep the lines of communication open

Unwrapping a surprise gift is always a pleasure.

Unfailing love is what God is.

Waiting in a doctor's office or waiting for a bus teaches me patience.

Walking is the most natural exercise there is.

Dying is just another dimension of life.

One day my vital functions will cease

My soul will go to Heaven or perhaps purgatory to live in God's Light forever.

No matter how I look at it life is a gift from God.

EVERY MINUTE

Every minute is precious

Every minute is a gift from God

The present moment, the now, is the most precious of all

It comes quietly then slips away

It's gone forever leaving nothing but memories.

Was it filled with laughter or wasted worrying about tomorrow?

Did it pass with love or tears of sorrow?

Was it used for saying a prayer or walking the dog?

Did you have lunch with a friend or cut someone's hair?

Was it spent making love?

Snatching an elderly woman's purse?

Were you doing the laundry or sitting in a dentist's chair?

Did you gaze at the stars above or give birth to a baby?

Someone I'm sure wrote a poem.

Perhaps someone watched her child take his first step

She listened with wonder as he uttered his first word

Someone learned a new skill or heard for the first time the song of a
bird

How will the present moment be used?

Will you read a book by your favourite author or search the Internet?

Will I listen to classical music on the radio or pay a debt?

Did you maybe meet a lover in the park?

Someone did housework then she cooked a gourmet meal for
company

I know that someone comforted a hurt child

Someone took inventory while his friend planned a vacation

Someone gazed at the night sky with awe and wonder

Someone else studied ancient civilizations

Perhaps the moment was used to forgive someone for a wrong long since past

I used it to start a new friendship

Did someone perform a daily task?

Was the moment used in letting go of a grudge?

A mother played solitaire then read her child a bedtime story

Someone made homemade fudge

Maybe you were just being still and giving thanks to the Lord above.

Was an important decision made in that moment?

Did you decide to lose a few pounds or to break a bad habit?

Your friend decided to do volunteer work once or twice a week

Someone decided to plant the seed of hope in someone's heart.

What a good way to use sixty seconds!

Did the moment pass by talking to an old friend or playing ball with the children?

Did anyone smile at a stranger?

Did anyone discover the adventure that waits around the bend?

Someone spent the moment fighting a war

Someone else joined a street gang

He bought a gun and then terrorized his neighbourhood

How will the moment be spent?

Will you learn to play the piano?

I want to learn how to play the guitar.

Did someone take care of a loved one who's ill or gaze at a distant star?

Will the present moment – now past – be spent in the bookstore?

Will you spend it in the library or buying new shoes?

Will I eat an ice cream cone or wait in the doctor's office?

Who will be at the bank?

Who will be in bed trying to get rid of the blues?

Was the moment spent in keeping a bedside vigil or lighting a candle?

Someone bought flowers for his spouse

I know someone who took a tour of the city

Someone else got a handle on a difficult situation.

My friend grieved for a loved one who died

The present moment can be spent in watching a new day dawn

On the other hand someone somewhere used it to plant a roadside bomb.

The moment can be used to plant a tree or to hug a child

You can watch a honeybee busy at work or see a butterfly land on a flower

A child pointed at a rainbow in the sky

I like to help protect wild animals and their habitat

My cousin likes to be a foster parent to an orphaned child.

There are countless ways to use the present moment

You can take the bag of clothes to the Salvation Army store

You can return the library books and mail the birthday card

He can rake leaves in the yard

Did you use the moment used to shovel snow?

Did you go ice-skating?

Did you win a race?

Did you stand at the door waiting?

Surely someone in a place across the sea went horseback riding

Someone wrote an examination and then visited the zoo

Someone told a friend I love you.

Did the moment pass by hiking through the woods?

Did anyone take delight in the autumn colours or attend a seminar?

Did anyone wish her brother and his wife a Happy Anniversary?

Someone used this moment to build a log cabin

To go to an auction sale

To begin packing for moving day

Was the moment used to send an urgent plea to God above?

Many people prayed that all wars would cease

Did anyone see the white dove of everlasting peace?

Did someone sit on the beach with a friend?

Did a newlywed couple leave for their honeymoon?

Perhaps a young woman received her first kiss

Perhaps someone rented a room.

Was the moment used for rock climbing or hitting a home run?

Did you play a round of golf or swim with dolphins?

A student jumped for joy that her assignment is done.

It is probable that someone attended a christening

Took his or her final vows

Acquired a new job

Slaughtered a cow

What a shame if anyone used those sixty seconds to hurt a friend

To spread a rumour

To have an abortion

To find out that he or she had cancer

Did someone fight a fire?

Save a life

Hug his child and kiss his wife

Where was the moment spent?

Were you on the subway or in a traffic jam?

On a plane headed east?

Were you at work or at church?

Were you in the hospital or at a party?

Was anyone at a funeral?

Someone was on a train headed west.

Was the moment spent on a park bench wrapped in newspaper?

I hope you weren't in a cardboard box on the street

There were lots of people in shacks, in houses or even in palaces.
Were you in a courtroom or in prison?
Someone I know was in a bar where good friends meet.
Did the moment tick by exploring the mysteries of space?
Did someone cry from a broken heart?
Did someone wake shaking from a nightmare?
Did someone else make a brand new start?
Someone had a dream
A dream about peace, love and a new birth
Someone else had a dream of evil
He planned to destroy the earth.
Was the moment used to attend an interview?
Did someone arrange silk flowers in a vase?
Did you remember to pick up the dry cleaning?
She prepared a romantic dinner for two
Maybe someone somewhere painted a picture
Someone else was caught stealing
Someone graduated from college
She wants to use her time healing.
Someone had a vision:
Healthy people, green grass, pure clear water
Crops growing in abundance
A world at peace
A world of unceasing love
Here, there and everywhere
Was the moment occupied by water-skiing?
Did you buy a motorcycle or go to a dance?
Did anyone go deer hunting?
Someone watched television
Someone performed an operation

Did someone play tennis or did she practice meditation?

Was the moment spent at the art gallery or at the museum?

I pray that it wasn't spent in the deep dark valley of depression.

Was the moment restful?

Was it filled with action?

Was it used wisely?

Was it lived with passion?

Eventually every minute ends up this way

From present to past

Every moment is precious

Every moment is special

No one knows which moment will be his or her last.

BITS AND PIECES

Bits and pieces of broken glass
Bits and pieces of a jagged rock
Bits and pieces of wood and cement
Bits and pieces of a woollen sock
Bits of flesh and drops of blood
Soak into the sand
Bits and pieces of body parts
That's all the remains of a man.
Why, oh why, why, oh why must human beings fight?
When, oh when, when, oh when are we going to get it right?
Pieces of unfulfilled dreams
Bits of a dying man's memory
Thoughts of his grandfather cross his mind
Someone he soon hopes to see
Pieces of a falling bomb
Sounds of a child's cry
A woman weeps in agony
As she watches her husband die
Bits and pieces of flesh and bone
When will we turn the bend?
Bits and pieces of lives unlived
Someone's son or someone's daughter
Lie beneath the shattered earth or in the muddy water
When, oh when, when, oh when will man's inhumanity to man stop?
When will we change a land of hate into a land of love?
When will human beings learn to live together in peace?
When will all wars cease?
When will we ever learn?

Bits of failure, bits of success
Bits of shattered dreams
Pieces of a broken heart
Nothing is the way it seems
Pieces of day, pieces of night
A mumbled prayer, a gasping breath
Is that really all that's left?
Bits of brown grass
Visions of his sweetheart's face
The fragrance of his favourite flower
A little bit of God's grace
Bits of knowledge
Pieces of dreams
Is she really holding his hand?
It's just his imagination
Bits of his life flow away
As he leaves this broken land
He sees bits of Light
Can this be Heaven's dew?
He hopes that the Light will grow stronger
He hopes that God's peace will shine through
He hopes those left behind will finally learn that war is not the answer.

PART FOUR

PART FOUR

TOO MUCH (1)

Too much violence

Too many gangs roaming the streets at night

Young people looking for friendship

They are seeking a sense of belonging

Some may find these things

Others will get a bullet in the gut.

Why can they not see that this path is wrong?

Why can't they see that this path leads to destruction?

Too many giant corporations gobbling up small businesses

Undercutting their prices

Putting the owners out of work

How do the giant corporations treat their employees?

How do they treat their customers?

Is bigger really better in the long run?

I for one don't think so.

Do you agree or no?

Too many homeless people

They live on the street or in shelters

In all kinds of conditions and in all types of weather

Where is the affordable housing?

The government promises affordable housing but I don't see any

All I see is condominiums and more condominiums.

Too many wars

Too many terrorists

Too many suicide bombers

Too many people dying

Their blood flows into the sand

It flows down the hill into the sewer.

Why do humans continue to kill each other?

Why do they do it?

Is it for freedom?

Is it for land?

Is it for oil?

Is it for revenge?

Too much injustice

Too much corruption in high places

Too many of God's laws being replaced by human laws

Too much money and too much power

Yes, too much money and too much power in the hands of a few men and women.

That power is being abused and misused

Money is promised for certain causes but suddenly the money is gone

The money was used for an individual's purpose

It should have been used for the good of the people and the country.

Too much pornography

Too much abuse of children and women

Too many elderly men and women being abused

They are forgotten by their families

They spend their last years alone or with strangers.

There is just too much violence all over the world.

Too many teenagers are dropping out of school

Too much garbage in our landfill

Not enough recycling being done

Too many walls around us

Too many fences

Too many are people making their own rules

Too many people are drowning their sorrows and their stress with the false gods of drugs and alcohol and sex

Too many people living in the darkness of depression are being ignored by the rest of the world

Too many people are having breakdowns unable to cope with all the stress in their lives.

There is just too much violence in the world

There are too many people with guns and other weapons

There are just too many wars in the world.

Will humankind ever let peace come?

FORGIVENESS

Why is it so difficult to forgive?
I guess it's much easier to bear a grudge
Against a friend, a sister or a brother
To forgive someone seems so easy
I just say I'm sorry and go on my way
There's a problem though
What's the point of saying the words if I don't mean what I say?
They have to be more than words
The words have to come from my heart.
It's not easy to forgive
I try but I still haven't seen the light
I've got to keep on trying
I've got to keep on working at it until I get it right.
Time marches on
Nobody knows how much is left
From the past come fond memories
Some memories I'd rather forget
Parents are people too
They do what they think is best
Can I remember it all?
Can I live in the present without regret?
I can.
Yes, I can.
I've forgiven this person from my heart
I've left the pain behind
Now it's time to forgive myself.

GO FOR IT! (2)

Why am I so serious when things get me down?
I make matters worse by wearing a frown
Nobody is perfect
Everyone makes mistakes
What does it matter if I don't get the breaks?
I laugh at my daydreams
It helps me to see
There is no one in the world exactly like me.
I have the power to change circumstances
It's all up to me
I have to take a few chances.
What's around the next corner?
It is frightening?
Is it real?
What does it all mean?
It isn't so bad
I'll just take a peak
Things are never as bad as they seem.
I won't bury my talent in the ground
I know that would be wrong
I'll keep working at it
I'll work at it until it becomes my song.
I know it's been said countless times before
Life is what I make it
It's not up to other people it's up to me.
My attitude and goals have changed
I'll put myself to the test
I won't wait any longer

It's time to pick myself up
It's time to shake off my gloom
It's time to sweep my doubts out the door
I'll use my big broom.

CHALLENGES(1)

I try to tell someone how I feel
I try to make them understand what for me is real
I want to do something that I've never done before
I have to find the courage to open up that door.
Take every opportunity as it comes day by day
Let my spirit guide me
Let love lead the way
Sometimes I'll have to take chances
Try not to pass any up
I'll work and play
Live and learn
Take one step at a time
Towards the winner's cup
I must give to life to receive something in return
All of my past moments are bridges that have burned
Sometimes I'm my own best friend
Sometimes I'm my own worst enemy
I'll learn to like myself
I'll learn to trust myself
Someday I'll unlock the mystery of me.

THE YEAR 2003 (2)

The year 2003 was a horrible year
It brought heat waves and sinus headaches
Thousands of people in Europe died
There were forest fires in British Columbia and California
There were floods in Quebec
From frustration and exhaustion people cried
Firefighters and volunteers worked diligently for days on end
They received a round of applause
They deserved much more than that.
There were green Christmases where white should have been
There were white Christmases where green should have been
People in these places hadn't seen snow for decades if at all.
There was the extremely fatal lung disease called SARS
Dozens of people died from this disease
Some people are still suffering today
Medical staff and volunteers everywhere were overworked
They tried to control the nasty bug
Thank God above for their courage and determination
They all need a hug.
There were earthquakes and mad cow disease
There were blackouts and melting polar caps
For many it was a year of sorrow
For others it was a year of doubt
There are still wars in many parts of the world
Especially in the Middle East
When, oh when, oh when will we ever learn?
When, oh when, oh when, we will tame the beast?
Now seven years later in 2010 not that much has changed

The world is still plagued with war

Global warming is still causing drastic changes in weather patterns

There are floods in one part of the world

Another part of the world is experiencing drought

Diseases such as bird flu are taking hold.

There is still violence, homelessness and violation of human rights

There are still terrorists and suicide bombers

People are still dying of malnutrition

They are still dying of HIV/Aids.

Is it my imagination?

Are things getting worse?

Greed, money, drugs and guns still rule the world.

Can we do anything at all to stop this madness?

I don't think it's my imagination

The world is self-destructing.

Have we not learned anything?

HERE WE ARE AGAIN

Here we are again
Right in the middle of living
Where we always are it seems
Trying to fulfill our dreams
Working on some scheme galore
Attempting to make more,
More money!
Here we are again
Caught in life's funny ways
Never minding the heat
Always wishing for something sweet
Yes, something sweet
Like a raise!
Here we are again
Whirling in a vicious circle
Money alone for money's sake
Leads us not to give but to take
I wonder if we'll ever see the light
I wonder if we'll ever
Wake up!
Here we are again
Always blaming others for our problems
It's not them you see
Don't you know that only we
Can set ourselves free
Individually!

DO YOU KNOW?

Do you know what time it is?
It's time for war to cease
Do you know what time it is?
It's time to live in harmony and peace.
Do you know what time it is?
It's time to love each other
Every sister, every brother
Do you know what time it is?
It's time to try peace.

HANDS

Hands that used to kill
Now caress and soothe and heal
Hands that were once covered in blood
Now build sand castles with his daughter
Hands that once held a machine gun
Now hold a crying child.
This is a vision I long to see
I hope I will some day.
Oh children of the Holy Land can you do this?
Can you break the cycle of violence that from day to day persists?
While the rest of the world prays for peace
You keep on killing each other.
I know I'm not from your culture or your land
Maybe I don't completely understand why you do the things you do
The thought crossed my mind though
Isn't there a better way to solve your differences?
Oh sons and daughters of war
Why don't you join your hands in peace with each other?

THIS MOMENT

Now is the time to be me
Now is the time to be set free
From the masks that I wear
From the grudges I bear
Why can't they just let me be me?
I must be the real me
I must do it now
I must spread my wings and fly
It doesn't matter what the world thinks
No matter how difficult it is I must try.
I must live, I must love
I must forgive and forget
I must live each moment without regret.
I want to explore all the adventures that life has in store
I see the darkness and the light
I know there are joys and sorrows behind every new door.
The present moment is the only thing that's real
The only time I have to show others how I feel
I must live every moment to the whole
I want my days to be full of showing others that life is worth living
Their gift is worth giving
I must live each moment as only I can until my breath is still.

HAPPY BIRTHDAY, CANADA – IT'S TIME WE GOT ALONG

Happy birthday, Canada
You are a land with many different people
Many different languages
Many different religions
Many different cultures
The people try to get along
Sometimes they do
When they don't that causes problems
Problems like vandalism
Problems like gangs with weapons roaming the street
Problems like racism
Problems like the murder of rivals
Yes, there are many different problems
Law enforcement is trying to solve them but it takes time
The victims of crime have to wait for justice.
Happy birthday, Canada
You are a beautiful land with wide open spaces
With rolling hills
With mountains and forests
With winding roads
You are a land of plenty.
Still many Canadians live in poverty
People like single mothers
People like the elderly
People like the homeless
Happy birthday, Canada
In some provinces communities have become ghost towns

148

There are no jobs

The jobs have all dried up

Businesses have gone bankrupt

Families have to pull up their roots and move

Some families decide to stay though

They are determined to help each other

It's a tough decision

Yet somehow they survive

Happy birthday, Canada

Many companies are downsizing

This action leaves the remaining employees with much more work to do

Some employees suffer burnout

They suffer nervous breakdowns from stress.

Some large corporations such as banks are making huge profits

Don't they know that people come first?

A minority of these corporations use money to help the poor and the homeless

Where does the rest of the wealth go?

It's a crying shame that it couldn't be more evenly distributed among the citizens of Canada.

Maybe someday is what I say

Maybe someday I repeat

Why not now?

What is the matter with right now?

Happy birthday, Canada

Despite your problems I wouldn't want to live anywhere else.

I wish a very happy birthday to my country, Canada.

TO MY PARENTS(1)

My Dad is ninety-three

My Mother is eighty-five

I feel so very fortunate that you're both still alive.

Through all the years you've given me

Love and wisdom and guidance

You still are

Sometimes we don't see eye to eye

Sometimes I don't listen

When I reflect on all you've done

My eyes begin to glisten with tears of gratitude.

A heartfelt thank you

Could never express my love for you

Listen, mother and father

I am very proud to be your daughter.

JOY

In the middle of the day
I'm lying on the bed beside my husband
I'm staring at the ceiling
I'm listening to the song on the rain on the window
Suddenly a feeling of deep joy overwhelms me.
In the middle of the night
I suddenly awake from sleep
The moonlight is shining through the window
I gaze at my husband's face
Suddenly a feeling of happiness surrounds me.

THE PATH

The path that I chose seemed so right

It seemed to clear

Why then did I end up in a web of disappointment, rejection and fear?

I must have taken a wrong turn somewhere

I sank deeper into despair

I knew that I had to change my ways before it was too late

I needed a friend but no one seemed to care.

They were all busy with their own lives

I struggled and I prayed

I prayed and I struggled.

Finally I stood on solid ground again

I said a prayer of thanksgiving to God

I was on a new path now

This path led to love and not destruction.

I was no longer lost.

Along this path I met a man who was heavily bowed down

For years he had been struggling both physically and emotionally

He too had been hurt in love just like I had been.

We talked for a while then he departed

The next day he phoned and invited me to dinner

We began to see each other frequently

I began to lose my heart

As the days and the weeks and the months passed

We fell head over heels in love

Deep down in our hearts

We both knew that this was the right choice

Neither of us was alone anymore

We had found a home in each other's arms.
We were part of each other's lives
Our love was strong and true
Soon we would become husband and wife
Our love was here to stay.

MY LOVE SONG

Ever since I met you
I've been very happy with everything we do
You are my one and only
You are my soul mate
Now and into eternity
I'll always love you
In good times and in bad times
I'll always be there for you
My love for you is true.
Take my hand and walk with me
Stay with me for all eternity
I give you my all
With you by my side I'll never fall.
For this love with you I'll share
Evermore and lasting care
For this love to you I give
For as long as I shall live
You and I will always be together for eternity
Take your hand and place it in mine
Together we'll stay for all time.

THERE WAS GOD

Before the first bird sang his sweet song
Before he spread his wings to fly
Before the first raindrops ever fell
There was God.
Before the first blade of grass grew
Before the first tree bore its fruit
Before the first flower blossomed
There was God.
Before the first star shed its light
Before the first wave lapped against the shore
Before the first horse grazed in the pasture
There was God.
Yes, there was God the Father
Creator of all things in heaven and on earth
Yes, there was God the Son
He died on the Cross for humankind's salvation
Yes, there was God the Holy Spirit
He gives us strength in times of trouble
Yes, there was God
God is three persons in one
God is the Blessed Trinity.
Before greed entered the Garden of Eden
Before the first lie was spoken
Before the first murder was committed
There was God.
There was God then
There is God now
There will be God forever.

GOD LOVES EVERYONE

The people at the post office
The people at the coffee shop
The people in prison
They are all children of God.
The people in line at the bank
The people at the airport
The people at the grocery store
They all belong to God.
The people at the bakery
The people at the doctor's office
The people in the apartment next door
They are all God's children too.
The people on the subway and the people on the bus
The people in the offices downtown
The people in hospitals and nursing homes
Every one of them is a child of God.
The homeless people on the street
The stranger that I meet
The children who play in the park
The people at the book store
They are all His children.
It doesn't matter what country we call home
It doesn't matter what name we give to God
God loves us
He loves every single one of us
God holds each one of us in His Hands.

I BELIEVE (1)

I believe in the sunshine and rain
I believe in the stars of night
I believe in the birds that sing
In the beauty of a wonderful sight
I believe in a tender smile
In a kind word too
In the sweet fragrance of a rose
I believe in you.
I believe in a soothing touch
In the rainbow above
I believe in the whispering breeze
I believe in love.
I believe in music
I believe in solitude
I believe in the Blessed Trinity
In the power of prayer too
I believe in laughter
In the dawn of each new day
I believe in hugs
In God's wondrous ways
I believe in second chances
I believe in a beautiful song
I believe in quiet places
I believe in righting a wrong.
I believe in friendship
That all wars will someday cease
I believe that some blessed day
The whole world will live in peace.

PROUD COUPLE (1)

A long time ago I set out upon the road
I was looking for love
I had been looking for love for quite a while
It seemed to have passed me by
Then I met you and I knew
I knew deep within my heart
I knew that our two lives would entwine.
Many years have passed since that day
Time keeps moving on
We still love each other
Our faith and our love grow strong
We've been through some calm waters
We've had some rapids along the way
We've had some good times
We've had times that we'd both rather wish away.
Sometime down the road
Sometime in the future
Maybe we'll look back on times and laugh
We'll smile about how we met each other
We'll recall how our love made the long wait worthwhile.
You and I together
Down the path of life we'll continue to go
We'll live and we'll laugh
We'll love and we'll learn
Time will keep moving on
Our love for each other will always be strong.

BEFORE YOU CAME

Before you came my life was empty
It was full of many things but not love
With you my heart is brimming over
It has new found thoughts of love.
Before you came my days felt long and dull
There was lots of rain but no sunlight
With you I look upon your face
Everything becomes so bright.
It lights a spark within my heart where embers ever glow
It fuels a fire deep within me
I just wanted you to know.
With you is heaven's play
I don't need a clock
Images of you start my day
In my heart, my mind, my thought
Now you are beside me in the morning
You're there at noontime and through the night
I'll be with you, my love, for the rest of my life.

A BIRTHDAY POEM

Happy birthday, my true love
You make my life complete
You are the one, the only man I love
You are the only one who makes my life so sweet
Another year, another birthday
Oh, what a happy time
You know that I'll always love you
In my heart and my soul and my mind

HOME

We have a little apartment to call home
A little space we've made our own
You and I together
To be in love forever
To share and to care
In every way to get better
There will be smiles
There will be tears too
That's the way life is
Love will give us strength
To face the coming years
Deep in my heart I know it's true
There will never be anyone else but you.
Just you, my love!

CONNECTIONS(1)

We are connected you and I

We are connected to the sky

We are all connected to each other and the universe

We are connected to the cosmos and to every creature on the earth.

THE DREAM (1)

Last night I tossed and turned
I dreamt strange dreams
Dreams so vivid I thought they were real
Dreams of war and bloodshed
Of horses neighing in pain
Of corpses left in the muddy field
Of disintegrating glass and steel towers
Of bombs raining from the sky
Of men and women and children left on the battlefield
They were left to die in agony
Of spirits who roam the world
They know that something is wrong
They refuse to rest in peace until their descendents get it right
Men and women and children who insist that war is wrong
Killing is wrong
Enough is enough!
All weapons of mass destruction are brought to one place
There they are destroyed.
There will be no more guns, tanks or poison gas
No more killing of our brothers and sisters
It doesn't matter if their religion is different from ours
It doesn't matter if they have something that we want
We will have to work in order to get it
No more kidnapping or torturing of hostages
No more destroying the earth and the land
No more polluting the water or the air
From this moment on it's going to be different
All the humans are going to live together in peace with each other

They are going to live in harmony with nature

Can we do it or is it just a dream?

Will we one day do it or will it always remain just a dream?

I woke up and stretched

I turned on the radio

I heard the announcer say that a suicide bomber had killed seven people.

I wept.

I was back in the real world.

ARE WE ALONE?

Time travel and UFO's
Other planets in our solar system
Lights in the night sky we don't understand
Comets, meteorites and black holes
Millions of stars winking above
Universes other than our own
Way, way, way, way, way out there!
They are countless light years away in deep space.
Are they all devoid of intelligent life?
Are human beings really alone?

TWO HOURS ON A FRIDAY AFTERNOON

I was sitting in the living room of my nineteenth floor apartment

I was reading my new novel

Odin, my dog, was having his afternoon nap.

Keith, my husband, was out doing some errands

Suddenly the silence was shattered

It was shattered by the ringing of the fire alarm

Odin jumped up

I snapped on his lead and grabbed my coat from the closet

We went out onto the balcony.

One fire truck came and then another

I stepped back inside for a minute and heard the announcement

"There is a fire on the sixth floor."

I heard the siren of yet another fire truck

That didn't help Odin any

He didn't like loud noises

He was trembling life a leaf.

More fire trucks arrived on the scene

I became concerned.

What was going on?

The next announcement said: "The fire is under control".

Why, then, were so many fire truck arriving?

Plus a police car and an ambulance

The ambulance, fortunately, wasn't needed!

The two cats, the three children and their mother were all alive.

They were helped from their smoke-filled apartment by the firemen.

Thank the Lord!

The small kitchen fire was out

There was a great deal of smoke damage.

When the alarm was turned off

Odin and I walked down the stairs to the lobby

It wasn't yet safe to use the elevators.

Odin had to pee very badly

Then we went to meet my husband at the bus stop which was three blocks away.

The firemen were still in the building when we returned

The lobby was full of tenants.

Finally, one elevator was released

The lobby slowly emptied.

Half an hour later we returned to our apartment on the nineteenth floor.

We were extremely thankful that everyone was all right.

COLLECTIONS

What do you collect?

Buttons

Fridge magnets

Stamps

Shot glasses

Teddy bears

Pens

Marbles

Antique dolls

Everyone collects something.

I collect words.

THE NEST: THE CHAIR

I put the old Lazy Boy chair out on the balcony

It stayed there for two years

It stayed in the wind and the rain and the snow.

One sunny day the thought crossed my mind that I should dispose of it.

I became busy with other things and didn't get around to it right away.

Later that day I saw a pigeon putting twigs under the chair

I couldn't believe it!

The idea was ingenious

She was building a nest under the chair.

The days passed but I didn't dare peak under the chair

I didn't want to disturb the pigeon.

I watched and I waited

Several days later I was rewarded

I heard the sound of baby pigeons cooing for their breakfast.

The birds are gone but the nest is still there

It's still there underneath the old Lazy Boy chair on my balcony.

CHANGES

Nothing stays the same
Not a blade of grass
Not a tree or a flower
Not a fast-flowing river
Not a field of wheat
Not the minutes of an hour
Everything changes in some way
The sky above
A drop of rain
The ground below
The wind that blows
A snowflake
Everything changes from day to day.
I watch them frequently
Daily if I can
I observe things to see the difference between yesterday and today.
And tomorrow?

THE SECRET

I stop and listen
I listen to the singing bird
He's serenading me
I stop and smell the fragrant rose
I watch the busy bee
I stop and look at the people around me
They pass me by without noticing
I sit on the park bench and observe them
The chattering of a squirrel catches my attention
I take a picture of him
I throw him a piece of bread
He grabs it and runs up the tree
I get up from the bench and walk to the grocery store.
I notice the pavement beneath my feet
The blue sky overhead
I don't hurry.
What's the rush?
I'm still learning the secret.

MEMORIES

It's been twenty-five years
Twenty-five years since we said our first "I love you!"
Twenty-five years since we decided to travel this road of love
We sealed it with "I do!"
They've been years of ups and downs
They've been years of smiles and frowns
There have been lots of changes but some things remain the same
We're still together, you and me
We've learned to live each new day as it comes by
We've learned to let the past go
It's already gone
Whatever has happened has happened
Nothing we do now can change it
We've learned not to hide love inside but to keep it alive.
We keep the good memories strong
We send the bad ones along.
Yes, they've been years of ups and downs
The roads of life have twisted and turned
The roads of love have taken us places we never thought we'd go
Through shallows, dangerous rapids and calm deep waters they have flowed
New sights and new sounds have made us laugh and cry
New friends have come into our lives
Old friends have passed on
Many of our bridges have been burned.
We've come a long way
We still have a long way to go
Next year we'll have new challenges to face

Ideas and attitudes and feelings will flow
Decisions will be made
Promises will be kept
We'll come through it all just like we have before
We'll come through it all with the help of God's Grace.

OUR ODYESSY

A few years after we were married my husband, Keith, and I drove west
to British Columbia

I remember the places we stayed

The towns and the cities that we passed through

I remember the friendly people

My fondest memory is seeing the Canadian Rockies for the first time

Such magnificence!

I remember our trip to England

It was my first time on a plane

I was terrified

There was no need to be

We arrived safely.

I remember the museums in London

The castles, the mystery of Stonehenge

A country so filled with history

I remember Canterbury Cathedral, Wren's architectural marvel.

Then we went by train to Scotland

Scotland!

I loved that place

Another country so filled with history

It's so difficult to take it all in.

The clans, the Highlands, the museums and the castles

The beautiful music of the bagpipes

Oh, the bagpipes!

Time to leave, time to board the plane for home

We'll go to Scotland again someday, I thought, and we did.

We're home again but not for long

Las Vegas was next on our list

We gambled some

We played the slot machines and won a little money.

We went by bus to see the Hoover Dam

That's really something to see

It's an extraordinary work of engineering.

The Grand Canyon and Dinosaur Caves Tour was utterly superb.

I must not forget our trip to Hawaii

The scenery, the waterfalls

The Halekea Crater, the Hana Highway, the Sunrise Tour

The Lakani Sugar Cane Train ride

The USS Arizona Memorial

The Nautilus Submarine Rider

They are all beautiful memories in my heart

There they will stay.

Two years passed.

Why don't we go east?

We rented a car and drove through Ontario and Quebec

On to New Brunswick we went by the scenic route

What a beautiful country road!

From New Brunswick to Nova Scotia

There it is!

Beautiful Peggy's Cove!

Beautiful people

We'll come back here one day, I thought, as we drove towards Toronto and we did.

We didn't take any more big trips for a while

Years go by

There are family problems and illness to deal.

In the year 2000 after a long bout with depression

Keith and I take another trip to Scotland

It was the best medicine ever and exactly what both of us needed.

The next few years bring more illness, moving, the arrival of a dog named Odin from the Toronto Humane Society and the death of my mother-in-law, Daisy.

When things settle down we decide it's time for another trip east

This trip will include Newfoundland

We rent a car and drive

Odin comes with us

We saw rainbows

We drove through rain and fog

We had long days behind the wheel

Finally we arrive in North Sydney, Nova Scotia

It is here that we catch the ferry for Newfoundland

Port Aux Basques, at last!

We drove to Cornerbrook to Grand Falls-Windsor

From Gander to St. John's

We took a bus tour of this city

Saw cathedrals, lighthouses and breathtaking scenery

Too soon it's time to board the ferry to carry us back to Nova Scotia.

We stopped at Springhill to see the Mine Museum

What an experience!

We took our sweet time driving back to Ontario

We stopped in Ottawa and took a tour of that famous city

We're home again!

Six months later, we fly to Fort Lauderdale, Florida

We rent a car from Alamo.

The next day we catch the cruise ship to Nassau

There we take a Glass Bottom Boat and Blue Lagoon Tour

Saw beautiful tropical fish and plant life

Now it's back to Fort Lauderdale and on to Orlando

We took in the show "Arabian Nights"

What a wonderful evening!

Two days later we fly back to Toronto

I'm glad to be home

To tell you the truth I really didn't like Florida all that much

It was just too hot for me!

We're already planning our next trip to Peru.

Yes, I said Peru!

Oh my, what can I say about this place?

It's mysterious and beautiful and full of history.

The Nazca Lines and the Pre-Inca Ruins were absolutely fascinating!

The Sacred Valley of the Incas and Machu Picchu were mysterious and exciting.

We're home at last

I'm glad to me home this time

I missed Odin.

The following year we took another long trip

This time it was to Portugal, Spain, France and Italy.

Fatima!

Beautiful, quiet and peaceful

From Fatima to Avila

Beautiful, rolling countryside, winding roads

In Avila, we saw cathedrals, statutes and stained glass windows

Now we're in Madrid!

Statutes, fountains, sculptured gardens, classical architecture

Spain to France

Narrow, winding mountain roads

Spectacular scenery

Florence is a beautiful city

We saw cathedrals, churches and statutes.

Rome!

Rome at last!

The holy city with its awe-inspiring statutes, churches, fountains and parks

I can't forget St. Peter's Square!

We have an early flight and now we're home

Home in Toronto!

Keith and I are both happy to be home this time

We're happy to sleep in our own bed and to see Odin again

Odin was happy to see us too!

GINA

A good neighbour
A wonderful friend
That's who she was.
A woman with a warm smile
A kind word for everyone she met
That's who she was.
In the last year of her life
She was ill with cancer
She bore it with patience
She never complained
A woman of faith
That's who she was.

DARKNESS

I let the stillness surround me
Let the silence envelop my soul
I breathed in
Breathed in god thoughts
I breathed out
Breathed out bad thoughts
Breathed in and breathed out
One, two, three times
No more thoughts entered my head
It was blank now
I let my limbs go limp
I floated away
I floated away into the darkness.

BLACKOUT

It was a beautiful August afternoon
We were in our nineteenth floor apartment
We were watching "Murder She Wrote"
I had to think of dinner soon.
Suddenly the television screen went dark
All the lights went out
The buildings around us were all the same
Odin began to bark.
I went and retrieved a flashlight
My husband got the battery-operated radio
We turned it to a news channel
We listened to it all night.
I fed Odin his dinner
Made tuna sandwiches for Keith and I
Two hours later Odin whined to go out
He really is a winner!
Down, down nineteen floors we go
The Golden Retriever and I
He does his business and plays for a bit
We have to climb those stairs he knows.
Being without power for three days
Sure changes the way you think
Lots of snuggling, lots of talking
God does work in mysterious ways.

SOUNDS OF LIFE

I hear footsteps on the stair
A child's laughter fills the air
A dog barking to get in
I hear the clothes dryer as it spins.
I hear the backfiring of a car
A train whistle blowing from afar
The squealing of a delighted child
I hear the howling of a wolf in the wild.
I hear the whispering of the breeze
The crying of a prisoner brought to his knees
The murmuring of love words during the night
I hear the screaming of a woman as she runs in fright.
I hear the waves lapping against the shore
The ripping of bone as it tore
The roar of a lion leaping at its prey
I hear the questions of a stranger lost in the maze.
I hear the sound of a plane overhead
The bomb as it explodes
In the wink of an eye a dozen humans lay dead
I hear voices praying for peace
They ask if they will ever tame the beast.
I hear a squirrel scampering up a tree
The buzzing of the busy bee
The pitter-patter of little feet
I listen to the words of Wisdom as she speaks.

TONIGHT

Tonight I see my love again
Tonight I see my man, my friend
Tonight I see love in your eyes
Tonight I hear your tender sighs.
Tonight I see your tender smile
It made all the waiting worthwhile
Tonight you hold me in your arms
Tonight I feel your tender charms.
Tonight I hold you close to my heart
Now I know we'll never part
Tonight we lay again side by side
Our love we no longer have to hide.

PART FIVE

MY UTOPIA(1)

Somewhere there is a beautiful world

Someone told me about this world

I don't know the location of this world.

In the world there is no war, no violence, no terrorism, no drugs, no street gangs, and no unwanted children

There is no global warming, no racism and no discrimination

There is no abuse of men or women or children

There is no cruelty to animals

People with physical or mental disabilities are accepted just as they are

They are part of the community.

There are no traffic jams

People travel by foot, bicycle, taxi, public transit or motorcycle

Some even travel by horse or dog team.

Homeless people don't exist in this world

There is more than enough affordable housing for everyone who requires it

There is affordable medical and dental care for the people who need such services.

There is no pollution of any kind

The people in this world do not waste either natural or human resources.

Unemployment is non-existent

Everyone who wants to work has a job at a fair wage

Jobs include anything from an auctioneer to a zoologist

In this world athletes don't make millions of dollars per season

The top salary is six-figures.

Each and every person no matter how young or how old is respected for his or her talent

No matter how small everyone's gift is welcomed without jealousy or envy

Everyone's gift is needed.

There are beautiful green spaces, parks and gardens

There are playgrounds for children

There are playgrounds for pets.

In this world people help each other

They work together to solve any problems that arise

Everyone is free to state his or her opinion

Unilateral decisions are not allowed.

Laughter and tears are shared as are triumphs and fears.

Strikes are absolutely illegal

There are no giant corporations to gobble up small family businesses

Companies remain small so that no downsizing or layoffs are necessary

Every working person receives a pay increase once a year

There are no exceptions.

In this world the health care system thrives

Doctors and nurses work in that profession because they love people and want to help them

The people agree on how high or how low administration fees will be.

Every teenager must complete high school

It is illegal to drop out

After graduation students decide if they want to attend college or university

Most students do want further education

If they want to enter into the family business and learn on the job that's okay too

Student fees are paid in full by the government of the day.

The people elect the government

If a politician makes a promise he or she can't keep they can be removed from the position by the people

The people are involved in every decision on how their world is run.

Every person regardless of age, creed, culture or lifestyle is treated with dignity and respect

This includes people who are living on the fringes of society and people who are dying in hospitals or nursing homes

All nursing homes in this world are inspected twice a year

So are educational institutions

So are apartment buildings

If major repairs are needed they are done immediately.

The people in this world use cooperation and compromise instead of force

There is competition but in a friendly way.

Cheating in any way is not permitted

There is no tax on essentials such as food or prescription medications.

No one is alone during a crisis

In this world people learn from each other

They celebrate life and death with each other

They live in harmony and peace with each other.

Wildlife is respected

People in this world do not encroach on wildlife habitat.

Nature is appreciated and respected

Nature is studied

People in this world live in harmony with mother earth

They don't try to control her.

Does this beautiful world really exist?

It's only in my friend's imagination.

Unfortunately, it's only in my imagination.

CHRISTMAS (1)

It's almost Christmas

What gift would you like to give?

What gift would you like to receive?

What gift would I like?

Nothing can compare to the priceless Gift that God gave to the world

God gave us the Gift of His Son, the Prince of Peace.

There was no peace when Jesus was born so long ago

There still isn't any peace in certain parts of the world

There are still hot spots of war, terrorism and dictatorship.

Why can't human beings cooperate with each other?

Why can't we use compromise instead of force?

Why can't we respect and appreciate each other?

Why are we so filled with greed, with anger and with rage?

Why can't we be filled with love, with awe and with wonder for each other instead?

Why can't we live in harmony and peace?

Why do we continue to destroy not only our own species but also other species that share this planet Earth with us?

How many thousands of years must pass before we get it right?

What is wrong with us?

Will we ever learn?

Another Christmas is almost here

Will this be the year that we let the Prince of Peace fill our hearts with love?

Will we let the rivers of blood stop flowing?

Will we let the circles of love and dignity and respect start growing?

Will this be the year?

Will we receive the message of love and joy that the Christ Child gives us?

Will we understand that this is God's only Son sent from Heaven above?

Will we believe that the Christmas message of peace is here to stay?

Even if we continue to ignore Him God will never go away

I have no idea when it will happen

I only know that some blessed day there will be peace throughout the earth.

Will this be the year?

IT'S NOT TOO LATE

It's not too late to stop the war

It's not too late to bridge the gap between the rich and the poor

It's not too late to admit that we're wrong

It's not too late to forgive the people who have hurt us

It's not too late for all of us to get along.

Why won't anyone believe me when I tell them that it's not too late?

It's not too late to compromise

It's not too late to stop telling lies

It's not too late to stop the greed

It's not too late to help our brothers and sisters in need

It's not too late for the politicians to use our tax dollars wisely:

To repair our roads

To save our children

To save our oceans

To save our forests

To save our wildlife

To stop cutting social programs

To fix our health care system so that every person has a doctor regardless of his or her economic status

To fix our transportation system so that there is more public transit and fewer cars on the road

To bring our troops home

It's not too late to save Mother Earth

It's not too late if we all work together

If every man and woman and child did his or her part

It doesn't matter how small his or her part may be

It doesn't matter how insignificant it seems

Every little bit helps

It's not too late to make the world a better place for everyone

It's not too late to change our way of thinking

It's time for the politicians to stop talking and to start taking action

It's time that every human being on this planet had the basic necessities of life

Why do countless numbers of humans have to eat garbage?

Why do they have to drink polluted water?

Why do they have to live in absolute squalor?

It's time!

No, it's more than time, for every person to be treated with respect and dignity

It doesn't matter what culture or religion or colour or sex they are

It doesn't matter what lifestyle they have chosen.

It's not too late to stop the torture and the violation of war prisoners

It's time to stop forcing other cultures to change their way of government

I've learned that I cannot change other people

I can't change anyone by force

I can't change anyone by persuasion either

I can only change myself

It took me many years to learn that.

When I did I found it much easier to accept people the way they are

When are the politicians going to learn this lesson?

Why is our military occupying a foreign country?

Think of how we would feel if a foreign country occupied Canada

I wouldn't like it one little bit

I don't think you would either.

How many more soldiers are going to return home in body bags?

How many more innocent victims are going to be killed?

Too many people have already died!

Too much blood has already been spilled!

Why won't anyone believe me when I tell them that it's not too late?

It's not too late to wean ourselves from our addiction to oil

It's time for more people to work seriously on finding other forms of energy that won't harm our planet

Wind power and solar power work

The problem is that they are still too expensive for the majority of people to use

We must find a way to lower the cost.

It's not too late to get rid of our pride

It's not too late to let our arrogance slide

It's not too late to admit that we're wrong

It's not too late to make amends for the destruction we've done

It's not too late to apologize

It's not too late to be reconciled

It's not too late to ask for forgiveness

It's not too late to accept forgiveness too

It's not too late to shake the hand of the person who was once our enemy

It's not too late for all wars to cease

It's not too late for the world to live in peace

Why won't anyone believe me when I tell them that it's not too late?

LISTEN, HUMANS

Calling all humans

People, please gather around and listen

Your height doesn't concern me

Neither does your weight

I'm not interested in your religion, your lifestyle or your place of residence

Those things don't matter at all to me

What matters is that we need to get together

Every one of us

The children, the teenagers, the middle-aged and the elderly

We need to communicate

We need to cooperate

We need to do everything in our power to stop war and violence and terrorism

These things kill

They kill not only us but they also kill Mother Earth

They are no good for anything.

Why do we allow these things to happen?

You ask a question and it's a good question:

Does it really matter if we stop war?

It just seems to be a part of life now.

Yes, you're right:

It does seem to be a part of life now but it shouldn't be

Neither soldiers nor civilians should die in such a horrible manner

Children shouldn't be left orphans nor women left widows

We must stop it!

We must stop it before we destroy each other completely

Before cultures are completely wiped out

Before Mother Earth is so badly wounded that she won't be able to recover

We must stop it before it's too late!

Let's stop it before this last chance has slipped away

Let's help each other

Let's help each other to overcome our differences

Let's learn about each other

Let's help each other to heal

Let's learn to respect each other

Let's learn to forgive each other

Let's bring peace to each other

Let's bring peace back to our earth.

SOMEWHERE THE TRUTH (1)

Somewhere between the earth and the sky
Somewhere between hello and goodbye
Somewhere between a smile and a cry
The truth will set the world free.
Somewhere between the mountain and the sea
Somewhere between the moon and the sun
Somewhere between the hell of war and the heaven of peace
The truth will set the world free.
Somewhere between the clouds and the rain
Somewhere between the joy and the pain
Somewhere between the work and the play
The truth will set the world free.
Somewhere between this minute and the next
Somewhere between the thought and the action
Somewhere between space and time
The truth will set the world free.
Somewhere between the dark and the light
Somewhere between the wrong and the right
Somewhere between birth and death
The truth will set the world free.
Somewhere between fantasy and reality
Somewhere between doubt and faith
Somewhere between ignorance and wisdom
The truth will set the world free.
Somewhere between yesterday and tomorrow
Somewhere between the depths and the heights
Somewhere between forgiveness and reconciliation
The truth will set the world free.

Somewhere between fear and trust
Somewhere between love and hate
Somewhere between the Tribulation and the Second Coming
The truth will set the world free.
Somewhere between the Alpha and the Omega
Somewhere between a stranger and a friend
Somewhere between the storm and the rainbow
The truth will set the world free.
Somewhere between the summer and the winter
Somewhere between spring and autumn
Somewhere between the sigh and the dream
The truth will set the world free.
Somewhere between the first and the last call for peace
Somehow between nations all wars will cease
Somewhere the world will meet the God of Love face to face
Some blessed day the truth will set the world free.

LOSES

Every time a wild animal or a flower or a fish is added to the Endangered
Species List

Worse, every time they become extinct

They are lost forever

Every time a river or a lake or an ocean becomes polluted with human
garbage

Do you know – do you realize – that everyone loses?

Every time a man or a woman or a child commits an act of violence

It doesn't matter if it's rape or murder

It doesn't matter if it's terrorism or kidnapping

It doesn't matter if it's arson or torture or bullying

What does matter is that it's wrong.

Every time a war is started

Every time it drags on and on and on and on

When there's no end in sight

Every time a soldier returns home in a coffin

Do you know – do you realize – that we all lose?

Every time the weather patterns change due to global warming

Every time a natural disaster occurs

Every time one person cheats another

Every time we don't respect a sister or a brother

Every time love takes a back seat to greed

Do you know – do you realize – that we all lose?

TOO MUCH (2)

Too much violence all over the world

Too many gangs roaming the city streets day and night

Young people looking for friendship and a place to belong

A few may find these things

Others may find themselves in prison

Others may die from a drug overdose

Why, oh why, oh why can't they see that this path is wrong?

This path will lead only to destruction.

Why can't they see this?

Too many giant corporations gobbling up small family businesses

Undercutting their prices

Putting people out of work

I don't like big box stores

I think that small family-run stores are better.

Too many homeless people

They live on the streets or in shelters

In all kinds of conditions and in all kinds of weather

Some die alone and cold and hungry during the cold nights of winter.

Where is the affordable housing that the government promised?

Why are there more and more and more condominiums being built?

People really can't afford them

That's how they get into debt.

Where is the affordable housing?

Too many wars

Too many terrorists

Too many suicide bombers

Their blood and the blood of their innocent victims flow into the sand
or down the hill into the sewer

Why, oh why, oh why do humans continue to kill each other?

Haven't we learned anything from World War I and World War II?

Why, oh why, oh why do we continue to kill each other?

Is it for freedom?

Is it for land?

Is it for oil?

Is it for religion?

Is it for revenge?

Too much injustice

Too much corruption in high places

Too many of God's laws being replaced by human laws

Too much money!

Too much power!

Yes, too much money and too much power in the hands of a few men and women

Both the money and the power are being misused and abused.

Too much pornography

Too much child abuse

Too many elderly men and women being abused during the last years of their lives

They are forgotten by their families

They are out of sight and out of mind

They spend their last years alone or with complete strangers.

There is just too much violence all over the world.

Too many teenagers dropping out of school

They won't get far without an education

Too much garbage in the landfill

Not nearly enough recycling, reducing and reusing being done.

There are too many walls around us

Too many fences

Too many prisons of our own making

Too many people are drowning their sorrows with the false gods of drugs and alcohol and sex

They play violent video games on the computer for hours

Too many people are living in the darkness of depression

Too many people are having breakdowns of one kind or another

They are unable to cope with the stress of their lives

There are too many people being ignored by the rest of the world.

Too many people committing suicide

They just can't take any more.

When, oh when, oh when will we stop abusing each other?

When, oh when, oh when will the bloodshed and the violence stop?

When, oh when, oh when will we let peace rule the world?

I'M COMING HOME

I'm coming home to you, she read
I've been away too long
My tour of duty is done
I'm coming home to you
Do you still remember our song?
I'm coming home to you
I'm not the same person I was before
The war has changed me
I've seen things that no human being should ever see
I've heard things that no human being should ever hear
I hope you understand
Am I still your special man?
Am I still your one and only?
Yes, she said, as he walked through the door
The letter was still in her hand
Yes, I still remember our song
Yes, you're still my special man
You're still my one and only
I'll help you in any way I can.
I know that the war has changed you
I can see it in your face
Your eyes don't smile any more
For the moment it doesn't matter
All that matters is that you're home now
You're in my arms
This is where you belong.

GOD OF MERCY(1)

God of Mercy

God of Love

God of Healing

God of Goodness

You sent Your only Son from Your throne above

He came willingly

He was born as a human baby

He was one of us in all things except sin.

God of Mercy

God of Peace

God of Strength

God of Might

God of Everlasting Light

Help us!

In the modern age we continue to crucify Your Son

We lie to each other

We kill each other

We try to control each other

We try to control nature too

We just have to be in charge

We don't want to obey anyone

We especially don't want to obey Jesus our Saviour.

We cheat each other

We abuse each other

We abuse nature too

The earth is polluted

The earth runs red with innocent blood

The poor and the weak

The homeless and the marginalized of society cry out for our help
For the most part we ignore them
We pass them by not even acknowledging that they exist
They do exist!
They are Your children, O God!
They belong to You!
God of Love
Help us!
Thousands of years have elapsed since Your Son walked the earth
He walked with people just like us
Yet now human beings do not remember His commandments
If we do remember them we choose not to obey them
Have we learned nothing since the world began?
God of Peace
Help us!
God of Love
God of Compassion
God of Wisdom
God of Light
Speak to our minds
Speak to our hearts
Help every individual do his or her part
To help heal the earth
To rid the world of the ravages of war
Help us remove from our lives the obstacles that keep us from You
Obstacles of greed and of ignorance
Obstacles of envy and competition and hatred
Help us replace these unwanted things with love
Help us replace them with communication and cooperation
With acceptance and understanding

God of Love
Help us!
Then maybe, just maybe
Future generations will know a world of peace.

IT'S STILL YOU (2)

Who makes me laugh with love?
Who makes me cry with love?
Who makes me smile with love?
Who makes me sigh with love?
It's still you, my husband.
Whose arms hold me all through the night?
Whose smile greets me at dawn's first light?
Whose voice sounds like music to my ears?
Whose face excites me whenever he is near?
It's still you, my husband.
Whose touch thrills me with delight?
Whose kiss makes my heart turn somersaults?
Who loves me despite all my faults?
Who makes me worry when he is late?
It's still you, my husband.
Who holds my heart in his hands?
Who tiptoes into my dreams?
Who has made my life complete?
Who is still my own true love?
It's still you, my husband.
You know that it's true
It's still you after twenty-five years together
It will be you right though eternity.

Who is my best friend?
Who is my confidant?
Who is my own true love?
Who will always be my man?
It's still you, my husband.
It will always be you, my husband.

COMPLETE

I walk through our apartment one room at a time
I touch familiar objects
A ceramic coffee mug
A china tea cup
A wool blanket
A solid wood telephone table
A cotton towel
A teddy bear
A glass vase
A silk flower
A pillow case
A knitted vest
A picture frame
A sheet of writing paper
The fur on Odin's head
They are all wonderful textures
They are all different
Not one of them is the one I seek.
I hear footsteps in the hall
A key turns in the lock
The door opens
My husband enters the room
He holds my hand
My fingers caress his cheek
That's when it happens
That's when I feel complete.

A SHORT LOVE POEM

When I hear my husband's voice
My heart takes flight
When I see his face
My heart overflows with delight
When I hold his body next to mine
I'm in heaven.

HERE, NOW AND FOREVER

These are just a few short lines of verse
They are dedicated to you, my love
We met somewhere in the great outdoors
In this God's beautiful and wonderful land
We fell in love
We promised to give each other all we had
To be there for each other
To have each other's best interests at heart
To hold each other in time of sorrow
To give each other our love no matter what the cost
Here, now and forever.
We two will share smiles and tears
We two will share joys and sorrows
We will share whatever life throws at us
We will work hard to make our dreams come true
Our fears will we face together
We will value our time
We will let our love grow
I need you by my side
You are my one and only
Here, now and forever.
Until the end of time, my love
I'll hold you in my arms
I'll whisper sweet words in rhyme to you
I never want to hurt you
I only want to care for you
I only want to share my life with you
I promise to love you

Here, now and forever.
I will cherish our love
I will appreciate the things you do
When things go wrong as they sometimes do
We'll face them together
Here, now and forever.

PROUD COUPLE (2)

Many long years ago I set out upon the road
I was looking for love
Not just any love but the right kind of love
I must admit that I had been looking for love for quite a while
It seemed to have passed me by
I shrugged my shoulders
I thought if it's meant to be then it will be
Time went by and still I waited.
The one cool winter's day something incredible happened:
I met you.
I could feel love in the air
Love was all around us
I knew you were the man for me
Deep down in my heart something magic happened
I had finally found the one I had been searching for
I had finally found my man
I knew even then that we would share our lives
I knew from the start that we were meant to be together.
Maybe sometime in the future
We'll look back on times and laugh
We'll laugh about how we met each other
We'll reminisce about how our love made the long wait worthwhile
You and I together
Down the path of life we'll go
We'll love
We'll laugh
We'll live
We'll learn

We'll cry some too
There's no doubt that we'll face challenges along the way
We'll overcome fears
Time will pass
Through everything our love will last.
Many years have come and gone since that day
Twenty-six years to be exact
We've been through some calm and peaceful waters
There have been some rough rapids along the way
We've had lots of good times
We've had some times we'd both rather wish away
Day by day time keeps moving on
We love each other still
Our faith has grown stronger
Our love has grown stronger too
Now and then I think about that enchanting day
The day that we met
The day I knew that we belonged together for life
The day I'll never ever forget.
There have been numerous changes since that day
Too many changes to count
Changes in jobs
Changes in apartments
Changes in lifestyle
Changes in health
Changes in attitude
Changes in hobbies too
We've had to make many difficult decisions
We've had to leave many things behind
Many new things have come into our lives

We didn't appreciate them at first but now we do.

There were times of encouragement

Times of frustration and desperate worry

Times of sorrow

Our love pulled us through

Our faith in each other helped too

Our faith in God kept us going

Helped us to take the next step

There were times of inspiration

Times of confusion and doubt

I recall times of awesome wonder and peaceful rest

Times of joyful celebrations and family reunions

Times of severe illness and bouts of depression

Times of hard work

Of uphill struggles

Of learning and adventure

Of yearning

Times of nothing but trouble

Times when nothing seemed to go right

Times when each of us needed an extra helping of patience

Sometimes we needed two or three extra helpings of patience!

Times of winding roads and broken dreams

Of sleepless nights

Times of goals achieved

Through the disappointments there was always love

Through the tears there was always joy

There is still love for us to share.

JESUS, MARY AND JOSEPH (2)

Her name was Mary
She was thirteen years old
She was a Jewish maiden from Nazareth
It was just an ordinary day
She was going about her daily chores
Suddenly the ordinary day turned into an extraordinary day
She saw an incredibly bright light
In the light stood a man only it wasn't a man
It was the Archangel Gabriel from Heaven
He had some awesome news for Mary
She would bear a Son and yet remain a virgin
Gabriel knew that this Jewish maiden had dedicated herself to God
She asked the Angel a question
She listened intently as he explained
Mary pondered Gabriel's words for a moment
He waited patiently for her answer
What if she refused?
What would happen then?
Would God find another Jewish maiden to bear His only Son?
Gabriel knew that this could not be so
He knew that God had chosen Mary from the beginning of time
Hers had been an Immaculate Conception
She had been born without sin
Mary still pondered and Gabriel still waited for her answer
The whole world waited for this maiden's answer
Mary said yes!
She knew what God asked of her wouldn't be easy but she believed
She believed in God's Word

She trusted in God

She said yes!

In that very moment the world's salvation was conceived in Mary's womb.

Blessed be Mary!

His name was Joseph

He was a Jewish carpenter from Nazareth

He and Mary were engaged

When he learned that Mary was with child he was upset

He was confused

He loved Mary with all his heart

How could she betray him like this?

When Mary described to Joseph what had taken place he doubted her

He just couldn't believe such a fantastic story

Only a fool would believe such a story

Joseph was no fool.

The Archangel Gabriel came to Joseph in a dream

Gabriel confirmed that Mary's words were indeed true

Joseph believed in God's Word

Joseph trusted God

He obeyed Gabriel and took Mary to his home as his wife.

Blessed be Joseph!

The days and the weeks and the months passed

With the other travelers Joseph and Mary made the long and the very dangerous journey to Bethlehem

The inns were all full that night

It was in a stable that the Holy Son of God was born

The animals were the first to see the Blessed Saviour

Choirs of Angels from Heaven sang to Jesus

The Angels spread the good news to the shepherds

The shepherds believed and hurried to see this wondrous Baby.

Blessed be Jesus!

Blessed be Mary His Mother!

Blessed be Joseph His foster father!

Blessed be God in Heaven for sending human beings such a marvellous gift of Pure Love!

A CHIRSTMAS POEM

Candles are burning

Hearts are yearning

A Holy Child is born tonight

Choirs of Angels are singing

Joseph is praying a prayer of thanksgiving

Mary gently places the Baby in a manger.

Angels from on high visit the shepherds

The shepherds are utterly terrified but they believe

They come to see this newborn Child

They come to see the Son of God

They adore Him.

Led by a star

A star that shines brighter than all the rest

A star that shines brighter than bright

A royal star

Wise men travel through the night

They ask in town where a wondrous Child may be found

Nobody can tell them

The royal star leads them to the stable

The King of kings was born in a stable!

They adore the Lamb of God

He was born in the flesh for you and me

He was born to set us free.

The donkey that carried Mary from Nazareth to Bethlehem nuzzles the Baby

Joseph`s faithful donkey brays

Joseph pats his head

The little lambs nuzzle Baby Jesus too

He is asleep on the fresh hay in the manger

He awakes and Mary holds him to her breast.

Love surrounds the earth

At the Holy Child's birth

The cold wind blows

The snowflakes fall

The shepherds return to the fields

They return to their flocks

Their hearts are filled with wonder at the sight they have seen.

In this day and age our minds are still seeking

Our hearts are still searching

They are still searching for something beyond the materialistic lives we live

God is here

God is always near

He is always knocking at the door of our hearts

All we have to do is to open the door and let Him enter in

We too can be filled with His Love.

PRAISES TO THE LORD

I wake up to hear the songbirds
They are singing praises to their Creator
The sunlight shines through the window
It throws shadows on the curtains and on the wall
Odin stretches and stands up
He shakes then jumps on the bed.
My husband is still asleep beside me
I sing silently my own praises to the Lord
To the Creator of Heaven and earth
I sing silently praises of thanksgiving
I sing silently praises of gratitude for this new day.

I BELIEVE (2)

I believe in the sunshine and the rain
I believe in the stars of night
I believe in the birds that sing
I believe in God's Everlasting Light.
I believe in a tender smile
In the sweet fragrance of a flower
I believe in the power of a hug
I believe in the beauty of each hour.
I believe in second chances
I believe in a beautiful song
I believe in quiet places
I believe in righting a wrong.
I believe in a soothing touch
I believe in the rainbow above
I believe in the whispering breeze
Most of all I believe in love.
I believe in the power of prayer
In every peel of laughter
In every falling tear
I believe in friendship
I believe that God is always near.
I believe in music
I believe in the dawn of each new day
I believe in flowing waterfalls
I believe in God's wondrous ways.

I believe in Guardian Angels

I believe that all wars will cease

I believe in forgiveness

I believe that some blessed day the world will be at peace.

GOD LIVES (2)

Some people say that God is dead
That He has no place in the twenty-first century
Some say that He never existed in the first place
I know better
I know that God lives!
God lives in the clouds
In every drop of rain
He lives in every butterfly
He's even in our pain.
God lives in the falling snow
In every beautiful flower
He lives in every shining star
He's in every minute of every hour.
God lives in the warm sunshine
In every blade of grass
He wants to live within our hearts
All we have to do is ask.
God lives in every loving touch
In every peaceful night
He's in every rainbow we see
He's in every dawn's first light.
God lives in the wind that blows
In every longing sigh
He's in every smile we send
He's in every newborn baby's cry.
God lives in all of His creation
In every gift we share
He's in every mountain

In every shimmering waterfall
God is everywhere!
God lives in every note of music
In every whispered word of love
He's in every peel of laughter
In every voice that sings
He lives in the homeless person on the street
In every stranger we pass by
God is above us
God is below us
God is before us
God is behind us
God is all around us
God surrounds us with His Love!
God lives!

I SAY A PRAYER

When I feel weak
When I feel blue
When I feel confused
I say a prayer to You, Lord Jesus.
When I can't sleep
When problems overwhelm me
When my tears drown me
I say a prayer to You, Lord Jesus.
When the shadows frighten me
When fear surrounds me
When darkness is all around me
I say a prayer to You, Lord Jesus.
I say a prayer to You, Lord Jesus
You alone are my God and my Saviour
I say a prayer to You to help me get through
Please lead me to Your Light.
Now I feel Your Hand on mine
Now I know that You are walking with me
You are with me every step of the way
Now I know that You were always there with me
Now I know that You always will be.

WORDS, WORDS, WORDS(1)

Words of acceptance
Words of wonder
Words of despair
Words of love
Words!
Words of hate
Words of rage
Words of mercy
Words of violence
More words!
Words of repentance
Words of forgiveness
Words of madness
Words of praise
Words of gratitude
Words!
That's all they are.
Just words!
Words of healing
Words of jealousy
Words of prayer
Words of death
Still more words!
Words of compassion
Words of comfort
Words of hurt
Words of joy
Just words!

Words of sorrow
Words of terror
Words of longing
Words of pain
More words!
Words between lovers
Words between friends
Words between fathers and daughters
Words between mothers and sons
Words between brothers and sisters
Words!
Words of the moonbeams
Words of the sunlight
Words of the raindrops
Words of the snowflakes
Words of the flowers
Words of the bees
Words of the birds
Words of the trees
Words of the earth
Words of the sky
Words of the thunder
Words of the lightning
Words!
Beautiful words but just words all the same
Words of goodbye
Words of happiness
Words of belief
Words of denial
Words of peace

What

What did you say?

Did you say words of peace?

Words of peace are so easily spoken and just as easily they are soon forgotten

They are such important words

I am waiting to hear the words of peace

So is the whole world

Words of peace that will last forever

Sounds of peace that will never fade

Words of truth

Words of justice

Words of love

Words of mercy

Words of forgiveness

Words of peace

What

Did you say words of peace again?

I hope and I pray that they aren't just words this time

Words of compassion

Words of cooperation

Words of laughter

Words of peace

Words of peace

You keep on saying words of peace

Words of peace don't mean anything

They are just words

Not this time!

Listen!

Listen and you can hear it

You can hear the words of peace
Listen to the beautiful sound it makes
Listen to the beautiful song it sings
One day it will cover the whole world
Some day
Only God in Heaven know when
Some day the whole world will hear the music of peace
Some day the whole world will dance to the music of peace.

REMEMBRANCE DAY

Remember the veterans
Their courage and their pain
Their broken limbs and shattered minds
The lives they fought to save
Remember the veterans
The sacrifices they made
They left home, families and friends behind
Our country, Canada, to save
Remember the veterans
Whomever you choose
By prayer or by ritual
Just remember them please.

SOME DAY

Over the hills and far away
That is where I'll be some day
Across the river on the other shore
That is where I'll be some day.
My soul will see the Face of Love
A Light so beautiful
A Light so pure
My soul will tremble at the Sight
Then my soul will praise and adore
The God of Love forever more
Such a Sight I hope to see
Such a Place I hope to be some day.

SENIORS

A noise invades my sleep

I open my eyes

It's five-thirty in the morning

It's still dark outside

My husband, Keith, is still fast asleep.

The noise is coming from our eleven-year old dog

He's whining to go out

I heave a deep sigh, get up and dressed.

The grass is covered with fallen leaves and raindrops

Odin does his business

Then he has a sniffing good time.

That's okay because I'm a senior too

It's my belief that seniors should be able to enjoy the simple pleasures of life

Sometimes that's all we have.

WHAT HAPPENED TO SPRING?

What happened to spring?
Why is it so late this year?
I wonder if spring is hiding somewhere
Maybe it's in the clouds
Maybe it's in the love light in my husband's eyes
What happened to spring?
Did the sun take it somewhere else in the world?
Come to think of it I haven't seen the sun for quite a while
I really wonder if spring got lost in my husband's sweet smile.
What happened to spring?

ONE LAST TIME(1)

It was a beautiful autumn day

I decided to walk to my favourite local shopping area

I usually take the subway

On this particular day I felt like walking

The things I saw on that walk:

Sparrows and pigeons eating in High Park

Squirrels chasing each other up a tree, across the branches and down again

Beautiful gardens

The flowers were alive with colour

As I was walking up the hill I saw an old friend

Someone I hadn't seen in several months

She recognized me as well

We stopped and chatted for a while

We promised to get together for lunch the next day

Then we parted.

We never did get together for lunch

That evening she died of a heart attack

I'm so glad that the Lord let me see her one last time.

SIXTY YEARS YOUNG

I've learned numerous things during my sixty years of living

Excuse me that should be sixty-one

I've learned that when I compromise then I get the best of both sides

I've learned that to be patient takes a great deal of practice

I've learned that to love and to be loved in return by the right man is worth more than gold

I've learned that after I forgave someone who really hurt me I was then able to forgive myself

I've learned that the simple pleasures of life are sometimes the best

I've learned that the power of prayer is indestructible.

I've learned that owning a dog is not only a joy but also a responsibility

I've learned that love is the answer to any question I'll ever have.

What else?

I've learned that accepting myself as I am with all my faults makes it much easier for me to accept other people as they are

I've learned that knowing something is wrong and doing it anyway could have very serious consequences

I've learned that trusting in the Blessed Trinity – the Father, the Son and the Holy Spirit – gives me strength

I've learned that letting go of old grudges relieves stress

I've learned that walking is the most natural exercise there is

I've learned that sleeping in my husband's arms is a thrill even after twenty-four years of marriage

I've learned that gazing at the night sky fills me with wonder

I've learned that meeting an old friend unexpectedly is always a wonderful pleasure

I've learned that love is the answer to any question I'll ever have.

THE LETTER

The letter I received recently from overseas made me sad
Tears fell from my eyes and ran down my face
A relative had died after a short illness
He's now buried beside his wife in an English cemetery
She arrived in heaven eight years before him
In the few months before his death he knew
He knew that it would soon be time to join her
Now they will be together for eternity.
My thoughts turned to the writer of this letter, my cousin
His soul is still burdened with sorrow
His mind is still filled with grief
He lost a father
His wife lost a friend
Memories of this wonderful human being will remain in their hearts
Memories will eventually bring them comfort.
Across the hundreds of miles from Canada to England
I'm sending my love and my prayers to my cousin and his wife
They will never forget their loved one
Neither will I
Sorrow will slowly fade
Some day memories will make them smile once more
Some day memories will bring them peace.

A MEDLEY OF THOUGHTS

Sometimes I feel so happy

My heart is so full of joy I feel that I can conquer anything

Suddenly a negative thought creeps into my head

The joy is gone

I get so discouraged and then I feel so mad

Sometimes I feel like I'm way up on cloud nine

At times I'm way down in the dust

Then I hear a friendly voice

Everything is fine once more

Sometimes I feel that I could do more

I could do more to help those people less fortunate

I do some

Is it enough?

No, it's never enough.

Sometimes I still experience the pain of separation from relatives who have died

They have gone before me to Heaven or maybe to Purgatory

I'm trying to live with my sorrow

I'm trying not to worry about what will happen tomorrow

I'm learning to concentrate on today

I'm learning to accept things as they come along

I'm getting better.

Thoughts of my dearly departed ones still wander through my mind

Thoughts of them still remain in my heart

I remember the love they gave me

I recall the things they taught me

I remember them

I remember every one of them

I love them still

I miss them and I always will.

Sometimes I think of the numerous experiences that have happened to me

The people I've met

The pain I've endured

The lessons I've learned

What lessons?

What experiences?

Well, let's see...

To compromise is much better than saying that I'm right all the time.

No one is right all the time.

To forgive the people who have hurt me sets me free from the heavy load of carrying grudges

To ask forgiveness of the people I have hurt takes courage but it's worth it

To travel to different parts of the world and see different cultures is an education

To frown when things go wrong only makes matters worse

Try to smile instead

To gaze at the night sky fills me with wonder

To ignore personal problems until they become overwhelming is a very bad idea

I've learned that simple pleasures are sometimes the best:

Simple pleasures like playing with my dog

Reading a good book

Listening to the radio

Arranging silk flowers in a vase

Visiting a sick friend

Playing solitaire on the computer

Keeping a scrapbook

Looking at my photograph albums

Having lunch with my sister

Spending a quiet evening with my husband

There are other things I think about sometimes

Other situations and other circumstances that influence all of creation

For instance?

Every time a wild animal becomes extinct and is lost forever

Every time a river or a lake or an ocean becomes polluted with human garbage

Do you know that everyone loses?

Every time a man or a woman or a child commits an act of violence

It doesn't matter what it is

Every time a war is started and there's no end in sight

Every time a soldier returns home in a coffin

Every time innocent blood is spilled

Do you know that everyone loses?

Every time weather patterns change due to global warming

Every time one person cheats another

Every time we don't respect a sister or a brother

Every time love takes a back seat to greed

Every time that competition is more important than cooperation

Do you know that everyone loses?

Sometimes I wonder about the mystery of life itself

The universe, the cosmos, is so vast

There are millions of stars above

Is there life on other planets?

I know that every minute that passes is a precious gift from God

Every minute comes quietly and then slips away

It is hardly noticed until it is gone forever

It is lost in the abyss of time

It can never return

It leaves nothing but memories behind.

Memories of old friends and the happy times we shared

Memories of places where I once lived

Jobs I once had

Places I once visited

Things I did that were wrong

Words I spoke when I should have kept silent

Collections of shot glasses, fridge magnets and stuffed animals that I bought and then sold

Books that I donated to the Library

Memories of the summers I spent at the cottage with my parents, my brother and my sister

Memories of the day when I met that special man who would become my husband

Our first kiss, our engagement party, our wedding day, our first apartment

I remember the day when we chose a dog named Odin from the Toronto Humane Society

How he changed our lives!

There are some memories I would rather forget

That's not possible

They are part of me too

Like my husband's illness and slow recovery

Like his bout with depression

Deep in the valley of darkness he was

He stayed there for a long time

Finally he evolved into the light; finally he began to get better

I remember my own bout with depression

I remember the day my mother-in-law died.

Sometimes I weep at the state of the world:

There are too many wars

Too much terrorism and too much violence

There is too much pollution of every kind

There is too much road rage

Too many people being overworked and underpaid

Too many companies downsizing causing great economic loss both to individuals and to the community

Too many young people committing suicide

Too much pornography

Too much hate

Too much greed

Too much need for power and money and guns and drugs

Too much innocent blood being shed

Too many street gangs

Too many orphans and widows in the world

Too much manipulation and too much corruption

Too much ignorance

Too much misunderstanding

Too much stress everywhere

Where, oh where, oh where, did the Garden of Eden go?

Then I look up and see a rainbow in the sky

I know that God is near

He is still watching over us

He is still helping us

He is still strengthening us

Most of all, He is still waiting patiently

He is still waiting patiently for humans to come to their senses

He is still waiting patiently for humans to learn.

It seems that we are very slow learners

When, oh when, will we learn to live in peace with each other?

When, oh when, will we learn to live in peace with nature?

When, oh when, will we learn to live in peace with the other species who share this planet with us?

Tell me when, oh when?

Tell me, when, oh when, will that happen?

SEASONS

The sidewalks are crowded with dogs and their humans

It seems that everyone is enjoying a reprieve from the bitterly cold weather

Fresh snow has fallen during the night

Paw prints and footprints are everywhere

Parents pull their children on toboggans

People both young and old walk to the outdoor rink

Their skates are slung over their shoulders

There are hockey games and snowball fights

Snowmen stand proud in front yards

The inevitable day arrives

The day comes when they start to melt one drip at a time

Winter is over!

Spring at last has arrived.

The sidewalks are filled with people

People and their dogs

I even saw a cat on a leash!

Parents are pushing baby strollers or pulling wagons

Some children have graduated and now have a tricycle

Some even have a bicycle with training wheels!

Listen!

I hear the sound of a motorcycle glad to be set free from hibernation.

Summer!

Summer is short but sweet

Time for shorts, tee-shirts and sandals

Maybe even bare feet

Time for lawn sales and picnics and days at the beach

The fragrance of beautiful flowers and freshly cut grass fills the air

Squirrels chase each other across front yards
Dogs chase the squirrels up the trees
Birds sing their beautiful songs
Bees and butterflies fly from flower to flower
People sit on park benches enjoying the gorgeous weather
Too soon summer turns to autumn
The nights start to grow colder
The leaves begin to change colour
They have their moment of glory
Now they die and fall to the ground
They are recycled back into the earth.
The sidewalks are filled with people out and about
Some are alone like me
Some are with family
Some are with friends
They watch the leaves change
They listen to the honking of the Canada Geese
They take delight in the last few days before the season changes again.

TEN SECONDS OF TERROR

Where did the bad thoughts come from?

Did they come out of nowhere?

Did they come from the depths of my mind?

Why did the bad thoughts return after all this time had passed?

I don't know the answer

I only know that they did.

My husband, Keith, and I were involved in an argument earlier that day

He wanted to go out to a political debate

I wanted to stay at home

After all, we had been to a political debate the previous evening

I didn't want to go out again

There was already too much going on:

I'd had a sinus headache all day

It was almost gone but it was still there

Besides that our dog, Odin, wasn't feeling well

I told my husband it was okay to go if he wanted to

I told a lie

It really wasn't

I wanted him to stay

He left.

A few minutes later it happened

The uninvited unwelcome thoughts arrived:

Ten seconds – maybe twelve – of suicidal thoughts

Maybe it doesn't sound like much

Believe me it was a lifetime

I glanced at the scissors then the knife

The knife would do a better job.

My hand reached for it

No, no, no, no, no!

My mind screamed

What in the name of Heaven and earth are you doing?

Do something else

Anything

Anything at all!

Hug the dog

Read a book

Say a prayer

Phone a friend

Play solitaire on the computer

Play solitaire the old-fashioned way with a deck of cards

Write a poem

There are dozens of things you can do

There is no reason for you to do that

Do you hear me?

Do you understand me?

It doesn't matter what you do

Just do something else

Anything else

Do you understand?

But don't, do you hear me, my mind shouted

Don't you dare pick up that knife and slash your wrists

Don't do it!

Don't do it!

Don't do it!

Don't you dare do it!

Odin would whine and bark until Keith got home

Keith would go mad with worry and fear

So don't do it!

For the love of God don't do it!

I didn't do it

I phoned a friend but got her answering machine

That didn't help

See, the bad thoughts insisted, nobody cares

I said a prayer

That did help

I took Odin for a very short walk

The fresh air helped clear my mind of the cobwebs and the bad thoughts

When we got home I played solitaire the old-fashioned way.

I AM

I am a foetus

I am a child

I am a teenager

I am a single young woman

I am a daughter, a sister, a friend and a cousin

I am a lover, a confidant and a wife

I am an aunt

A great aunt now

I am blood, flesh and bone

Spirit too am I

Am I right or am I wrong?

Am I weak or am I strong?

Am I good or am I bad?

Am I happy or am I sad?

Am I a loser or am I a winner?

Am I a saint or am I a sinner?

At one time or another during my life I have been all of those.

I am an apartment dweller

I am a dog owner

I am childless

I once longed to have a child but it wasn't meant to be

I used to cry about it but now I understand

I am an insurance clerk

A buyer and seller of antiques

A library worker

That was several years ago

I am retired now.

I am still a daughter, still a sister and a friend

Still a wife and a lover
I am a poet
A traveler
A student of life
I thank God for every day
I thank God for who I once was and who I am now
I thank God for what He has given me
I thank God for every day that my husband and I spent together.
Every day I learn something new about life
Every day I learn that every day is a blessing
I am grateful
I am in awe of God's Love and Mercy
I am glad that I am me.

THIS PRECISE MOMENT

This rock

This tree

This snowflake

This sea

Each one is unique

It will never be seen in the same way again as it is seen in this precise moment.

This butterfly

This flower

This raindrop

This hour

Each one is unique

It will never be seen in the same way again as it is seen in this precise moment.

This sky

This moon

This street

This room

Each one is unique

It will never be seen in the same way again as it is seen in this precise moment,

This laughter

This face

This smile

This place

Each one is unique

It will never be seen in the same way again as it is seen in this precise moment.

This pain

This bird

This leaf

This word

Each one is unique

It will never be seen in the same way again as it is seen in this precise moment.

This moment

This care

This sunrise

This prayer

Each one is unique

It will never be seen in the same way again as it is seen in this precise moment.

This star

This fear

This joy

This deer

Each one is unique

It will never be seen in the same way again as it is seen in this precise moment.

This child

This right

This day

This night

Each one is unique

It will never be seen in the same way again as it is seen in this precise moment.

This road

This book

This dog

This look

Each one is unique

It will never be seen in the same way again as it is seen in this precise moment.

This play

This work

This dust

This earth

Each one is unique

It will never be seen in the same way again as it is seen in this precise moment.

This friend

This breath

This life

This death

Each one is unique

It will never be seen in the same way again as it is seen in this precise moment.

This journey

This love

This beauty

This dove

Each one is unique

It will never be seen in the same way again as it is in this precise moment.

JUST WAITING (2)

A book
It's just waiting to be read
A teddy bear
He's just waiting to be bought
A lonely heart
It's just waiting to be touched
A child
She's just waiting to be hugged
A Saviour
He's just waiting to be loved
A dove
He's just waiting to cover the earth
How He longs to cover the earth with His blanket of peace.

SOLITUDE

You and I are alone together

We are listening to the music

We are listening to the beautiful music

The beautiful music of the shimmering flowing waterfall is serenading
us

It's a moment away from the crowd

It's a moment away from the busyness of life

It's our moment of inspiration.

DEAR GOD

Dear God

I thank You for this brand new day

For my family, friends and relatives I do pray

I say a prayer for the sick and the lonely

I say a prayer for the homeless, the unemployed and the elderly

I say a prayer for all those who have no one left to pray for them

I pray for peace in the world with all my heart

I pray that all evil and all greed will soon depart

I say a prayer for all the victims of war and terrorism

For all those who are still crying

For all those who are still trying to forget the horror of 9/11

I pray for all those who have died and for all the souls in Purgatory

May they one day see the shining Light of your Love.

Dear God

Blessed Trinity

Father, Son and Holy Spirit

I thank You for guiding my footsteps this day

I thank You for showing me the way

For carrying me when I was weak

For strengthening me when trouble came knocking at my door

Now I pray that You will watch over me as I sleep

Please watch over me this night

Please watch over the people I love

Keep us safe from harm

Lead us all to Your everlasting Light.

THE HEAVY GRUDGE NOW GONE

I don't know why I still carry this heavy grudge
All it does is weigh me down
I should get rid of it
I should let it fall from my shoulders
I should bury it in the ground.
I've been carrying it for so damn long
I can't even remember when it began
I can't even remember what it was about
Now it feels a part of me
I just can't seem to let it go
I guess I'll never be free.
Yes I can let it go
I can!
I can and I will!
My mind repeated the words
I can and I will!
The words flowed through my mind again
Let it go!
It's not doing me any good at all
It's making me blind to the beauty around me.
I'll write a letter to her
This woman who used to be my friend
I'll pick up the phone and maybe we can talk
We can try to put the cruel words behind us
The words that led to the moment of anger
The moment of anger that ruined our friendship
We can put them in the past where they belong
They don't belong in the present or in the future

They belong in the past

That's where I'm going to put them

That's where they are going to stay.

I wonder if she remembers it

It's more than time to let it go.

Today is a brand new day

Today is pristine and untouched

Today is the day I'll open up the door of my heart

If I can't open the door of my heart then I'll open a window

Today is the day I'll get rid of this heavy grudge

I'll get rid of it once and for all

Today is the day!

Yes, today is the day!

I looked up her number

I was amazed to find that she lived less than seven blocks from me

Maybe I had passed her on the street

Maybe we had even talked before now and not realized it

My fingers were trembling as I dialled her number

She answered and recognized my voice

We began to talk as if nothing had happened

As if nothing had come between us

Soon enough the memory of that night slipped out

We talked about the heavy grudge

We looked at it every which way

We argued about it

We each admitted that we had hurt each other

We agreed to bury the heavy grudge

We buried it right then and there

We buried it right where we stood

Then we laughed.

I felt better and so did she
Unbidden the question came to mind
Why on earth had we wasted all those years?

GOODBYE IRELAND

Goodbye. Ireland

The two weeks passed far, far too quickly

We and our traveling companions explored your country roads

Winding roads they were

We saw breathtaking scenery

We had dinner in both pubs and castles

We saw churches and cathedrals

We saw mountains and rivers and beautiful gardens

We observed sheep, cattle and horses grazing in your green fields

We met wonderful and friendly people

We heard stories about your villains and your heroes, your politicians
and your poets

We saw Irish dancers and heard Irish music

Now beautiful emerald isle

Now sadly it's time for us to depart

Goodbye, Ireland

Memories of you will remain in our hearts.

PART SIX

ODIN (2)

When we went to the Toronto Humane Society
My husband, Keith, and I were planning t get a puppy
After talking to us the man said no
We didn't know what to do
He thought for a minute and then he said:
"Have I got a dog for you!"
That's how Odin came into your lives
He was a five-year old dog
We had no idea how much he would change us
We had no idea he would act like a god
He's a Golden Retriever
He's a gorgeous shade of red
We just can't get angry with him when he jumps up on the bed.
When he wakes me in the morning whining to go out
I get dressed in silence
Sometimes I want to shout
When he's done his business
He wants to go for a longer walk
Here's no way to resist those brown eyes
So again we go around the block.
When I come home from doing errands
Odin greets me with wagging tail
Keith and I can't leave him alone for long
His bark would become a wail
It seems that we've had him forever
He fits in so well with us
There's no doubt that he's our dog
He's part of the family

He's definitely one of us.

The years passed

Before we knew it Keith and I had celebrated our sixty-first birthdays

Odin had celebrated his twelfth

Three months elapsed

One morning I woke up and noticed something unusual

Odin had peed on the floor

He had never done that before

During the day he whimpered a lot

Was he in pain?

He wouldn't eat

He didn't want to go for a walk

Was our Golden Retriever sick?

We took him to the veterinarian

She examined him

The news wasn't good

His kidneys were failing.

The choice was ours:

She could give Odin the operation or she could put him to sleep

Keith and I discussed it

We knew this moment would come

We just didn't expect it to come so soon

We did what was right for our four-legged companion

We didn't want him to suffer.

I believe Odin knew

Before he went to sleep for the last time

He looked at Keith and then at me

He was saying thank you

I know you are my humans

I know you will miss me

I will miss you too
I wish I could stay with you longer
Thank you for understanding
Thank you for letting me go
I know how difficult it is for you.
With gentle caresses and with tears
We said goodbye to him
He licked our linked hands
He closed his eyes
A few seconds later Odin was gone
He was now in dog heaven.

ODE TO AUTHORS (2)

I love books
I don't think that I could live without books
Books surround me
They encircle the room
Which one will I read next?
Which one will I choose?
I have murder mysteries
They make my blood run cold
I have enchanting love stories
They involve knights of old.
I have words of great mystics
They make my soul fly
I have words that inspire me
Sometimes they make me cry.
Words on a page
They can take me to another place
They can even take me far away
They can take me light years away to outer space.
From the depths of their imagination
Storytellers write
Whenever the muse is with them
Be it day or be it night.
Books make good friends
Anytime or anyplace
No matter where I am
If I'm on the bus I have a book with me
If I'm at the Laundromat I have a book with me
No matter what the weather

On a cold rainy day
I stay in my apartment and read
On a beautiful sunny day
I sit on a park bench and read
I've read numerous books
I've enjoyed every one of them
Thank you, authors!

IT SHOULDN'T MATTER BUT IT DOES (2)

It shouldn't matter if the colour of my skin is white or black or red or anything in between

It shouldn't matter if I sleep on the street or in a comfortable bed

It shouldn't matter if I wear a turban or a woollen hat on my hair

It shouldn't matter if I am mentally or physically challenged or never have a care

It shouldn't matter if I'm married or single

It shouldn't matter if I'm always early or always late

It shouldn't matter if I never ride a horse or lace up a pair of skates

It shouldn't matter if I'm a genius or have little education

It shouldn't matter of I'm a carpenter or the president of a nation

It shouldn't matter if I'm fat or slim

It shouldn't matter if I have children or if I'm childless

It shouldn't matter if I live in a country that's cold or one that's hot

It shouldn't matter if I wear hand-me-downs or buy my clothes brand new

It shouldn't matter if I'm a chatterbox or never express my point of view

It shouldn't matter if I live in a house, in a shelter or in a cardboard box on the street

It shouldn't matter if I have a friend or nobody at all to meet

It shouldn't matter if I'm a teacher or work at the bakery making buns

It shouldn't matter if I'm a newborn baby or if my life is nearly done

It shouldn't matter if I'm a bad person in prison or a child playing in the park

It shouldn't matter if I'm retired from the work force or a new graduate trying to make my mark

These things really shouldn't matter at all but they do

Not one of them should really matter at all but they do.

What should matter is that each and every one of us knows who or she really is

Each and every one of us is a human being

We are made in the image and likeness of God

Each and every one of us is a unique individual

Each and every one of us was put on this earth for a specific purpose

Each and every one of us is a child of God

Do we treat each other so?

Do we treat each other with respect?

Do we treat each other with dignity?

Do we help each other?

Do we forgive each other?

Do we love each other?

Do we treat each other with friendship?

We are all children of God

It doesn't matter what name we call Him

It doesn't matter about the colour of our skin

It doesn't matter about our creed

It doesn't matter about our lifestyle

It doesn't matter about our race

What matters is that each and every one of us knows who he or she is

Each and every one of us is a child of God

Some day each one of us will see God's Face.

LOVE'S SONG (2)

Love's song is a warm embrace
Love's song is a smiling face
Love's song is a guiding light
It shines through the darkest night.
Love's song is a faithful friend
He's always waiting around the bend
Love's song is music so sweet
Love's song is the tear we weep.
Love's song is a whispered word
Love's song is a singing bird
Love's song is a flowing stream
Love's song is a waiting dream.
Love's song is a star so bright
Love's song is doing what's right
Love's song is a quiet space
Love's song is a sacred place.
Love's song is sung with courage
The music is different on every page
Love's song is together growing old
Love's song is much more than a band of gold.
Love's song is one of caring
It doesn't matter what the cost
Love's song is one of sharing
We share joy and pain
We share whatever comes along
It doesn't matter what's lost or what's found
Love's song is one of understanding
Love's song is one of truth.

Love's song grows deep within

The music is sometimes loud

The music is sometimes dim

Love's song is what my parents had

Their love song flowed through 67 years of marriage

A few days ago God called my Dad home

My Dad is waiting in Heaven for his wife, his best friend and his soul
mate

My mother was all of these things to him

Even though he's gone their love song is here to stay

Their love song will never fade away.

THE DREAM (2)

Last night I couldn't sleep
I tossed and I turned
I dreamt strange dreams
I dreamt weird dreams
Dreams that seemed so real that I thought I was actually there
Dreams of bloodshed
Dreams of war
Of horses neighing in pain
Of men screaming in agony
Of corpses left in the muddy fields
Of disintegrating glass and steel towers
Of bombs raining from the sky
Of men and women and children dying in absolute agony
Dying in absolute agony on the battlefield
Dying in horrible agony in their homes
Of spirits who roam the world
Of spirits who know that something is terribly wrong
Of spirits who refuse to rest in peace
They refuse to rest in peace until their descendents get it right.
These are spirits of men and women and children
Spirits who know that war is wrong
Killing of any kind is wrong
Violence of any kind is wrong
Terrorism of any kind is wrong
Enough is enough!
Do you hear us?
Enough is enough!
Do you hear us?

We will haunt you day and night
We will haunt you until you get it right
Do you hear us?
Enough is enough!
All weapons of every kind are brought to one place
There they are destroyed
Every one of them is destroyed
There will be no more guns
No more tanks
No more poison gas
No more killing our brothers and sisters because they are different
Their religion or their skin colour
Their culture or their lifestyle
Does it really matter?
No more kidnapping
No more torturing prisoners
No more destroying the earth
No more polluting the land and the air and the water
No more!
Do you hear us, people?
No more!
Enough is enough!
Do you hear us?
We are spirits of past wars
War doesn't solve anything
Haven't you learned that yet?
Do you hear us?
Will you listen to us, people?
Will you learn from us?
Will you learn from us before it's too late?

Do you hear us, people?

Enough is enough!

From now on it's going to be different

From this moment on it's going to be different

Do you hear us?

All of humankind is going to live in peace together

There will be no more war of any kind

Humankind is going to live in peace with each other

We are going to live in harmony with nature

We are going to live in harmony with all the other species who share this planet with us

The spirits are shouting now

They are shouting at us

Do you hear us, people?

Do you hear us?

Are you listening?

Enough is enough?

This can be done

It's not impossible if you cooperate with each other

You can do it!

It is not just a dream

Enough is enough!

SOMEWHERE THE TRUTH(2)

Somewhere between the earth and the sky
Somewhere between hello and goodbye
Somewhere between a smile and a cry
The truth will set us free.
Somewhere between the mountain and the sea
Somewhere between the moon and the sun
Somewhere between the hell of war and the heaven of peace
The truth will set us free.
Somewhere between the clouds and the rain
Somewhere between the joy and the pain
Somewhere between the work and the play
The truth will set us free.
Somewhere between this minute and the next
Somewhere between the thought and the action
Somewhere between space and time
The truth will set us free.
Somewhere between the dark and the light
Somewhere between the wrong and the right
Somewhere between life and death
The truth will set us free.
Somewhere between fantasy and reality
Somewhere between doubt and faith
Somewhere between ignorance and wisdom
The truth will set us free.
Somewhere between yesterday and tomorrow
Somewhere between the depths and the heights
Somewhere between forgiveness and reconciliation
The truth will set us free.

Somewhere between noise and silence
Somewhere between love and hate
Somewhere between the Tribulation and the Second Coming
The truth will set us free.
Somewhere between the Alpha and the Omega
Somewhere between a stranger and a friend
Somewhere between the storm and the rainbow
The truth will set us free.
Somewhere between the summer and the winter
Somewhere between the flower and the tree
Somewhere between the sigh and the dream
The truth will set us free.
Somewhere between slavery and freedom
Somewhere between the east and the west
Somewhere between humans and nature
The truth will set us free.
Somewhere between the first and the last call for peace
Somehow between nations all wars will finally cease
Somewhere the world will meet the God of Love face to Face
Some blessed and awesome day the truth will set us free.

NOTHINGNESS(2)

The snow fell on my uncovered head
The cold wind burned my bare hands
I walked then I ran
I didn't care where I was going
It wasn't important to me
I just had to get away
I had to get away from that place.
The city streets were far behind me now
It was almost dark
My legs grew weary
My breath came in gasps
I tripped and fell
I seemed to have fallen into a dark emptiness.
Soon the snow covered me like a blanket
My body seemed to dissolve into nothingness
My mind tried to forget that my Dad had died the previous day
My mind tried to forget but it couldn't.

DIFFERENT PEOPLE(2)

How can you know how I feel unless you ask me?

How can you assume to know my thoughts?

What gives you the right to judge me?

What gives me the right to judge you?

Does it matter if my way of living is different from yours?

We are not all the same

We are not perfect either

We all make mistakes

Each one of us looks at life differently.

We are all coming from a different path

Who is to say who's right and who's wrong?

We live each day according to what we believe

Everyone we meet influences us in some way

Every new adventure makes us grow

Sometimes we cry more than we laugh

Sometimes we work so much that there is no time for play

Sometimes we learn the hard way that our priorities were wrong

Sometimes we don't live but we just survive.

There are some things that I don't understand

Why do we destroy our home?

Why do we destroy our world?

Why do we destroy the earth?

Why do we abuse life?

Life is our most precious gift, isn't it?

Sometimes we have storm clouds

Sometimes we have rainbows

Why can we not accept ourselves as we are?

Why can we not accept others as they are?

Each and every one of us is a unique individual
Why do we change just to please someone else?
Why do we not know the value of our own worth?
Each person on this earth is an individual
We are not all the same
There is no one else like you in the entire world
There is no one else like me.

CHALLENGES(2)

Now is the time to be me
Who else on earth can I be?
Now is the time to be set free
Set free from the masks that I wear
Set free from the grudges I bear
If I don't do it now when will I do it?
Now is the time to be the real me
I'm tired of trying to be someone I'm not
I must spread my wings and fly
It doesn't matter what the rest of the world thinks
It doesn't matter how difficult it is
I must try.
I must live my life as only I can
I must love
I must forgive
Yes, I must forgive those who have hurt me
I must accept
Yes, I must accept forgiveness from those I have hurt
I must learn
Yes. I must learn from the mistakes I've made
I must live
Yes, I must live each moment without regret.
I must live each moment in the present
What else is there?
There's nothing else
Yesterday is gone
What's done is done
What can I do about it?

Nothing
It's gone forever.
Tomorrow is far away
There's only today
That's all there is.
I will let my spirit guide me
I will let love lead the way
I see the darkness and I see the light
I see the joys and I see the sorrows too
I see the pleasure and I see the pain
I see the loss and I see the gain
I will take one step at a time
One step at a time is all that I can do.
I know I must give to life
Only then will I get something in return
All of my past moments are no more
Their bridges have been burned
The present moment
Yes, the present moment is the only thing that's real
It's the only time I have
The only time I have to show others how I feel
Sometimes I'm my own best friend
Sometimes I'm my own worst enemy
If I learn to accept myself as I am I'll eventually unlock the mystery
I'll unlock the mystery of me.

WORDS, WORDS, WORDS(2)

Words of acceptance and words of wonder
Words of love and words of joy
They are just words.
Words of hate and words of violence
Words of frustration and words of desperation
They are just more words.
Words of repentance and words of forgiveness
Words of madness
Words of praise and words of gratitude
They are just words.
They are just more words.
That's all they are.
Words of healing and words of prayer
Words of jealousy and words of envy
Words of life and words of death
They are just more words that someone speaks.
Words of compassion and words of comfort
Words of happiness and words of sadness
Words of hurt and words of disappointment
They are just words.
They are nothing more than words.
Words of sorrow and words of pain
Words of anger and words of terror
Words of longing and words of tenderness
They are just more words.
Words of encouragement and words of inspiration
Words of tolerance and words of pity
Words of humour and words of wit

Words of wisdom and words of blessing
They are just more words.
That's all they are.
Words of justice and words of power
Words of destruction and words of despair
They are just more and more words.
Words between lovers
Words between friends
Words between mothers and sons
Words between fathers and daughters
Words between brothers and sisters
Words between mothers and daughters
Words between husbands and wives
Words between fathers and sons
Words are spoken all the time.
Words of the moonbeams
Words of the sunlight
Words of the raindrops
Words of the snowflakes
Words of the bees
Words of the flowers
Words of the birds
Words of the trees
Words of the butterflies
Words of nature
Words of the humans
They are nothing more than words.
Words of the earth
Words of the sea
Words of the mountains

Words of the rocks
Words of the sky
Words of the thunder
Words of the lightning
Words of the rainbow
Words somehow lost in the tears of goodbye.
Words of sadness and words of denial
Words of faith and words of peace
What?
Did you say words of peace?
Words of peace are such beautiful words
They are so easily spoken
They are just as easily forgotten
They are such important words
I am waiting to hear the words of peace
I know that the entire world is waiting too
I want to hear words of peace that will last forever
I want to hear words of peace that will never fade away.
Words of trust and words of honesty
Words of justice and words of truth
Words of falsehood and words of danger
Words of love and words of hope
Words of mercy and words of forgiveness
Words of peace
What?
What's this?
Did you say words of peace again?
I hope that they are not just words this time.
I pray that it is so.
Words of compassion and words of cooperation

Words of laughter and words of love
Words of hope and words of reconciliation
Words of peace
Words of peace
You keep on saying words of peace
Words of peace don't mean anything
They are just words like any other words.
Not this time!
They said words of peace and then they took action
They took action to make it so
No, they didn't take an action of war like has happened for countless
years
They took an action of compromise
They took an action of cooperation
Listen!
Listen and you'll be able to hear it.
You can hear the words of peace
Listen to the beautiful sound it makes
Listen to the awesome song it sings
One day it will cover the whole world.
Some day
Some blessed and beautiful day
The whole world will hear the words of peace
They will be words of true peace.
Some day
Some blessed and beautiful day
The whole world will hear the music of peace
It will be music of true peace.
Some day
Some blessed and beautiful day

The whole world will dance to the music of peace
It will be a dance of true peace
It will be a song of everlasting peace
Yes, it will be a dance of everlasting peace.

CHRISTMAS(2)

It's almost Christmas

What gift would you like to give?

What gift would you like to receive?

What gift would I like?

Nothing and I mean nothing anywhere in the whole world can compare to a Gift we already have

All we have to do is to accept it

It is the Gift that God gave all of humankind

God gave us the Gift of His only Son, Jesus by name

Jesus, the Prince of Peace

Why is there no peace then?

There was no peace on earth when He was born so long ago

There still is no peace in certain parts of the world

There are still hot spots of war, hot spots of terrorism and hot spots of dictatorship.

Why can't human beings cooperate with each other?

Why can't we compromise?

Why can't we respect and appreciate each other?

Why are we so filled with greed and anger and rage?

Why can't we be filled with love for each other instead?

Why can't we be filled with awe and with wonder?

Why can't we live in peace and in harmony?

What is wrong with us?

What is wrong with us?

Why do we continue to destroy not only our own species but also the other species that share this planet with us?

This used to be a beautiful planet

It is not so beautiful now.

What is wrong with humankind?

Why do we think that we have the right to control everything?

We don't have such a right!

We don't.

How many thousands of years must pass before we get it right?

Why can't we learn from our mistakes?

Will we ever learn?

Will we learn before it's too late?

Another Christmas is almost here

Will we let the Prince of Peace fill our hearts this year?

Will we let the rivers of blood stop flowing?

Will we let the circles of love start growing?

Will this be the year?

What about the circles of respect and gratitude and appreciation?

Will this be the year?

Will it?

Will this be the year that we receive and accept the message of love that the Christ Child gives us?

Will this be the year that we understand that this is God's only Son?

He willingly left His Father's throne in Heaven above

He was willingly born in a cold and dark manger

Will this be the year that we believe that the Christmas message is here to stay?

God will never go away

Even if we continue to ignore Him God will never give up on humankind.

I SEE YOU(2)

I see you.

Do I really?

Do I really see you?

You are just another human being

You are a stranger to me

You have your pain and your joy

You have your dreams and your hopes

You are a unique individual

You have your talents.

Do I really see you?

You are just another person

You are just someone else taking up space on this earth.

In reality I don't see you at all

All I see is a stranger

Maybe I want to get to know you

Maybe I don't

All I see is another person

Just another person getting in the way of my life

If I saw you

If I really saw you

If I really saw you as you are

You with all your worry

You with all your loneliness

You with all your frustration

You with all your personal problems

You with all your commitments

If I looked into your eyes instead of looking at the ground

If I looked at your face instead of looking straight ahead

Is it possible that you could make my own life better?

I'll never know

No, I'll never know until I take the time to see you

I'll never know until I take the time to see you as you really are.

KEEP IT SIMPLE(2)

Keep it simple.

Three little words that are so very difficult to do

So very difficult to do in this world we live in

This world of terror, this world of war, this world of violence

People are so confused

They are so frustrated

Some are so easily led astray

They don't know whom to trust

They don't know whom to believe.

People are anxious

They are overworked

They are stressed out

Some use drugs and alcohol and sex to ease their pain

Some are unable to cope with life

They commit suicide and end it all

They will never see another sunrise or another rainbow

They will never hear again their daughter's laughter.

Pre-teen gangs wander the streets with weapons

They do violence to other humans

They destroy property just for the fun of it

They don't know whom to trust

They don't know whom to believe.

Recently two big financial institutions were on the verge of bankruptcy

They had to be bailed out by the government

Now people are worried about their future

Their jobs may be at risk

How could this happen?

Was it wrong information?

Was it greed?

The government spends millions of dollars fighting a war

A war it probably won't win

A war we shouldn't even be involved in

How many families have lost a beloved father or son?

Too many!

How many families have lost a precious mother or daughter?

Too many!

How many more soldiers will return home in body bags?

Too many!

How many more innocent people will be killed?

Too many!

Keep it simple.

Is such a thing actually possible in this world?

Is it?

Why is war still raging in the land where Jesus once walked?

When will it end?

Bodies of the wounded and dead soldiers lie on the ground

Blood and guts are everywhere

Another suicide bomber explodes

She kills a dozen people

A dozen more are maimed for life

Why are we so full of anger?

Why are we so full of hate?

Why are we so full of greed?

We don't know whom to trust.

We don't know whom to believe.

Keep it simple.

I will try

You never know but it just might work

What will you do?

Will you try too?

What do you think?

Will humankind really do that some day?

Will we finally get it right?

Will we finally learn to keep it simple?

Is such a prospect possible?

I hope so.

I believe so.

Will we learn to live in peace as God intended?

I hope so.

I believe so.

What a beautiful and blessed day that will be!

TO MY PARENTS(2)

Oh my dear parents
I love you both so deeply
Dad, you are in Heaven now
You were ninety-six when you died
Mother, you are eighty-eight
Things will be so different for you now
Together we will get through the grief
Together we will survive.
Through all these years you've given me so many things
Love, guidance and wisdom
Many times we didn't see eye to eye
Many times I didn't listen to your advice.
Now I reflect on all you've done, Dad
My eyes begin to glisten with tears
They are tears of sadness, yes
They are also tears of gratitude and appreciation
I love you, Dad
I will miss you.
A heartfelt thank you could never express
My deep love for you and mother
I am very proud mother and father
I am very proud to be your daughter.

PART SEVEN

PART SEVEN

SIMPLICITY

Simple

Uncluttered

Non-complex

That's how I like my life to be

It wasn't always so

I used to have the bad habit of making my life complicated

Much more complicated than was necessary

My life was cluttered with material possessions that I never used and
didn't need

Past regrets were weighing me down

There was no reason to hang onto them

I learned to let them go

I learned to let go of the past

It's gone

Whatever has happened has happened

There's nothing at all I can do about it now

Nothing, that is, except to learn from my mistakes

Nothing, that is, except try not to make the same mistake again

That isn't easy but I do.

These days I try to keep my life simple

I try to practice positive thinking

I am grateful for my blessings

I explore my senses

I embrace my present

I embolden my future by the actions I take today

I do my best to keep my life simple.

THANKSGIVING DAY

What am I thankful for on this Thanksgiving Day?

On this Thanksgiving Day of 2008

I thank God for my health

For the love I share with my family and my friends

For the love I share with my husband

I am thankful for every smile, every hug, every kiss and every touch.

I thank God for the blue sky above

For the green grass below

For springs flowers and for songbirds

I am thankful for the precious memories of my life

They are kept safe in my mind and in my heart

I am thankful for beautiful sights and peaceful nights

I thank God for all the people who have touched my life

For all those who have helped me through times of trouble

Yes, there have been times of trouble for me

Times of sorrow and times of woe

Times when my life was put on hold

A huge mountain of worry enveloped me

How would I get out of this mess?

I've lost count of the times I've asked myself that question

There have been times of illness

Times when I thought I wouldn't see the light of day again

I did though.

I'm here!

I'm still here!

I thank God that I'm still here!

There were times in the recent past when the whole world was in terrible turmoil

Everything was turned on its head

Everything was upside down

Everything was backwards.

When two big financial institutions collapsed

When jobs disappeared at an alarming rate

When people just didn't know what to do

They didn't know if they would survive the situation

There didn't seem to be any way out of it

There was no way around it or through it either.

The entire world was in a crisis

With prayer

With hours and hours of discussion

With hours upon hours of discussion and compromise and prayer

Things got better

They got slowly better

At a snail's pace things got better

People breathed a sigh of relief

Thank You, God!

I thank God for my country

My country Canada

For wide open spaces

For mountains and waterfalls

For trees and wildlife and flowers

I thank God for the diversity of people who live here.

I thank God for my Guardian Angel

He or she guards me

He or she guides me through life's winding roads and detours and valleys

Most of all I thank God for His precious Love

For His Mercy and for the Gift of His Son

Without God, where would I be?
I would probably still be on a path that led to destruction and fear
With God's help I got off that path
That path led to nothing but a dead end
Thank You, God, for showing me the path of love.

BLOOD IN THE SNOW

I don't remember falling
One minute I'm watching my dog play in the snow
The next minute I'm flat on my face
My foot must have found a small patch of ice
I don't remember standing up
My Guardian Angel must have helped me
Blood was running down the right side of my face
It dripped onto my coat
From there it dripped to the ground
Odin and I walked back to the hotel room
I wiped the blood from my face
There was a deep cut above my right eye
My husband, Keith, called the person on duty at reception
This kind gentleman gave us directions to the Peterborough Hospital
Thank the Lord it wasn't very far
We made it there without incident
Odin was a very good dog
He stayed in the car
He could sense that something was amiss.
Keith and I waited in the emergency department
The minutes ticked by
They turned into hours
One, two, three hours passed
Still we waited
Patiently we waited
Another hour slipped by
I was now growing impatient
Finally a doctor saw me

He closed the cut.

Keith and I left emergency

I knew that I would be all right

Odin was overjoyed to see us.

It was very late when we arrived back at the hotel

Keith, Odin and I were tired

We were together though

We were together and to me that was all that mattered.

IT'S JUST YOU

It's not the words you say to me
It's not the things you do
It's not the love you give to me
My man
My love
My husband
It's just you.
It's not the promises you keep
It's not the tears you make me weep
It's not that I know you're there for me
My man
My love
My husband
It's just you.
It's not the smile on your face
It's not that we have our own little place
It's not your arms or your warm embrace
My man
My love
My husband
My Valentine forever
It's just you.

LOVE

Love is mysterious
Love is overwhelming
Love shines in your eyes
Love shows in your smile
Love trembles in the expression on your face.
Love takes you beyond yourself
Love takes you into someone else's life
Love can make you wait forever until the right person comes along
You will somehow know
You will know with the first kiss
Your heart will overflow with delight
You will think of that person day and night.
Love can make you change your ways
Love will brighten up your darkest days
You don't understand what's happening to you
It's so strange what's happening to you
It's strange but it's wonderful too
You just don't understand.
Why is there magic in the air?
Why is love all around you?
Why do you feel the way you do?
Why does everything look so beautiful?
In the very deepest part of you
You know that this love is for real
You know that this love is meant to be.
Alas I must tell you
Love can sometimes be frustrating
Sometimes love can be complicated

Sometimes love can even be cruel
Sometimes love won't put you up on cloud nine
Sometimes it will throw you into the pit instead
It will make a fool of you
Sometimes this is true
What do you do then?
Perhaps the person wasn't right for you
I was hurt in love before I found my true love
Before I found my soul mate love treated me badly
He was hurt in love too
Let your heart heal then try again
I believe that there is someone for everyone
It took me a long time before I found my true love.
True love is a mystery
True love is overwhelming
True love changes your life forever
True love is well worth the wait
True love never comes too early
It never comes too late
True love comes exactly on time.

I REMEMBER

When we walk hand in hand
When we leave footprints in the snow
When we watch the autumn leaves fall
I remember.
When I feel your gentle touch
When I feel your lips on mine
When you reach for me during the night
I remember.
When I feel your arms around me
When you chase my bad dreams away
When I lie awake and watch you sleep
I remember.
When one of your headaches comes on
When it puts you down for the day
When we have to cancel the plans we made
I remember.
When you go out and forget the time
When you make me worry
When I feel your love around me
I remember.
I remember why I fell in love with you
There's no one else like you
There's no one like you in the entire world
No other man would ever do.
When we agree to disagree
When we make a difficult choice
When I know that no one loves me the way you do
I remember.

THE KIND OF DAY

It's raining outside
It's foggy
It's windy
It's the kind of day for staying indoors
The kind of day for watching television
For listening to the radio
For reading a good book
For snuggling with my husband
The kind of day for us to enjoy each other's company
It's the kind of day for us to share.
It's sunny outside
There's a beautiful blue sky
It's warm
It's the kind of day to be outside
For sitting on the park bench
For watching the squirrels
For listening to the songbirds
For feeding the sparrows and the starlings
For observing the parade of people as they hurry past
For my husband and I to hold hands
The kind of day for us to delight in each other's company
It's the kind of day for us to share.

MOTHER'S DAY

This is a wish for my mother
This is a wish for my sister
This is a wish for all my friends
To all those who are blessed with motherhood
I hope your day is filled with smiles
I hope it is filled with unexpected surprises
I hope it is filled with special moments
Moments that will remain in your heart as precious memories
I hope your day is filled with love.

THE LORD OF ALL CREATION

I see the flashes of swift lightning

I hear the roaring thunder in the distance

I feel the cool rain on my face

I praise the Lord of all Creation for His Glory.

I hear the buzz of the busy bee

I smell the sweet fragrance of a flower

I see the autumn leaves floating to the ground

I praise the Lord of all Creation for His Glory.

I hear the whisper of the breeze

I see the Canada Geese on the wing

I see a Monarch butterfly

I praise the Lord of all Creation for His Glory.

I see the sunlight shining on the lake

I see the full face of the moon

I feel the green grass beneath my bare feet

I praise the Lord of all Creation for His Glory.

I feel the darkness of the night surround me

I hear the classical music on the radio

I feel my husband's arms around me

I praise the Lord of all Creation for His Glory.

YOUR BIRTHDAY

Your birthday is a day to celebrate you
Nobody else but you
Your uniqueness
Your accomplishments
Your talents
Your courage
Your friendship
Your love
Even your frustrations
Even your disappointments
They all belong to you
No one else do they belong to
There is no one else like you in the entire world
The world contains millions of people
Still there is only one you
Your single steps
Your mind
Your leap of faith
Your body
Your spirit
Your life
Your birthday is for you to celebrate yourself
So let's celebrate!
Let's celebrate the day that you were born
Let's celebrate you!

REJOICE

When all the angry bitter words have been spoken
When they are long forgotten
When all the fighting is through
When all the war machines have rusted in the sand
Will we then let peace rule the earth?
When all the soldiers have passed on
When a new generation of children has been born
When they begin to treat each other differently
Will they give peace a chance to rule the earth?
When they don't want to fight any more
When bitter enemies slowly become friends
When they finally give peace a chance
Then the whole world will rejoice
Then peace will rule the earth.

CHLOE

She's a little dog
She has brown eyes
She has butterfly ears
She was born in the country
My husband and I bought her
She now lives in the big city of Toronto with us
So many changes the little dog has been through
So many changes for her new humans too
She still has a few fears
She still has a few things to learn
We are working on those together
Chloe, my husband and I
She will be okay
She will be our four-legged companion for many years to come
She is with us to stay
This little dog
This Papillon
This little Papillon named Chloe

TIME MARCHES ON

Time marches on
It doesn't wait
No matter what you do
No matter where you are
Time disappears minute by minute.
Time marches on
The days, the months and the years go by
A little while ago you were just a baby
How did you so quickly become a teenager?
The birthdays keep coming
The birthdays keep going
The sun rises
The sun sets
Another day is gone
Time marches on.
Time marches on
You remember when you were first married
You remember when your daughter was born
It was a remarkable experience
Now she's a bride
Now she has a daughter of her own.
You are now long retired from your teaching career
You're not retired from life yet
Now you have new dreams
You have now choices to make
You have new adventures to consider
New friends have come your way
Time marches on

Time still marches on.
Time marches on
It doesn't matter if you're a newborn baby
It doesn't matter if your life is almost through
Sooner or later it will happen to us all
Time will simply run out for you.
Time still marches on.

SO MANY REASONS

There's something I want to tell you
The words are simple
The words are honest
The words are true
They are meant just for you.
I love you for so many reasons
For your smile
For your touch
For the way you care
For the love we share
I love you for just being you.
I love you for so many reasons
For helping me to see the world differently
For encouraging me to do things I didn't think I could do
For making my life better
I love you for just being you.
I love you for so many reasons
Some are big
Some are small
Sometimes there's no reason at all
All the reasons are wonderful just like you are
I love you for just being you.

REMEMBRANCE

In his mind he wanted to forget

In his heart he wanted to remember

He remembered those horrible days and years of the Great War

The war that was supposed to end all wars

He saw the bombs raining from the sky

He saw the broken bodies and the flailing limbs of his friends

He saw their blood flowing everywhere

He heard their agonizing screams of pain

He heard again the mumbled prayers of the wounded and the dying

Thousands of men fell in the battle

Thousands remained to face the enemy.

On this Remembrance Day he turned ninety

He relived all the emotions and all the anguish he had lived through
then

He was one of the fortunate ones though

He was never taken prisoner

He survived to come home.

Yes, he came home

He came home to his beloved wife

She saw the sadness in his eyes

She heard him screaming in the dark of night from the terrible
nightmares

She heard him sobbing in pain from the loss of his friends

She heard him praying for strength.

Life went on but it wasn't the same

Still they made it work

She also prayed for strength

She comforted him as best as she could

She asked him if he wanted to talk about it

He shook his head

No!

It was too horrible, too frightening, for a woman to hear

She knew the war had changed him

She knew that the anguish in his soul sometimes overwhelmed him

She knew that even all this time later he still carried scars that she couldn't see

She comforted him with her love

It was enough to make him forget for a while

He knew that her arms would always welcome him

He knew that he wasn't alone

His faithful wife hadn't left him

She was still here

He was grateful for her.

The war to end all wars didn't end all wars

After all these years there were still wars going on

When will we learn?

He'd asked himself that question a million times

When will we learn?

When will we learn?

Oh dear God in Heaven when will we learn?

Why does history keep on repeating itself over and over and over again?

Why can't we change it?

When will we ever learn?

Now war had taken his grandson

His grandson had been killed in Iraq by a roadside bomb

Today the body of his grandson would be driven along the Highway of Heroes

A hero he was

He had fought for his country
He had paid the ultimate price
The war to end all wars didn't.

JOY IS EVERYWHERE

Joy is in the skies of blue
Joy is in our love so true
Joy is in the stars of night
Joy is in God's unfailing Light.
Joy is in a friend so rare
Joy is in those who care
Joy is when we right a wrong
Joy is when we all get along.
Joy is in the flowers of spring
Joy is when the angels sing
Joy is in a smiling face
Joy is in a warm embrace.
Joy is when there's no more greed
Joy is when we plant love's seed
Joy is when enemies become friends
Joy is when all wars end.
Joy is in the rainbow above
Joy is in the mystery of God's Love
Joy is when love reigns on earth
Joy is when we accept our worth.
Joy refuses to be kept down
Joy simply spreads itself around
Joy is when you hold my hand
Joy is when we understand.
Joy is when the walls of hate fall
Joy is when we hear God's call
Joy is in a butterfly's wings
Joy is in the praises of gratitude we sing.

Joy is in the gifts we receive
Joy is when God's Word we believe
Joy is when all wars and violence cease
Joy is when there's everlasting peace.

CHANGES

Nothing stays the same forever

Not a blade of grass

Not a tree

Not a flower

Not a river

Not the minutes that daily pass

Not you

Not me

We all change in some way

Everything changes every day.

The sky above

A drop of rain

A snowflake that falls

The ground below

The wind that blows

The pain within my heart

Everything changes from day to day

So does everyone I know

I watch them frequently

Daily if I can

I observe things around me

I observe my loved ones too

I notice the difference between yesterday and today

What will tomorrow bring?

No one knows

I'll take it one step at a time

I'll face it with courage

I'll get through it just like I always do.

MY WISH FOR YOU

My wish for you is a Merry Christmas
A very happy New Year too
May you be blessed with good health
May good friends surround you
May you prosper in all that you do
I wish a joyful Christmas to you.

A NEW YEAR

Another year is ending
It was a year of changes
The move from Toronto to Peterborough
The severe illness and slow recovery of my Dad
He didn't recover completely though
One evening my Dad died peacefully at home
He simply closed his eyes and went to sleep.
The purchase of a second Papillon dog named Tristyn
He will be a companion for Chloe
In England the birth of a son for my cousin and his wife
A New Year is just beginning
What will this New Year bring?
Will I be a kinder person?
Will I be more forgiving too?
Will I learn to be more patient?
Will I celebrate life in a healthier way?
Will I keep the promise I made to myself to lose ten or fifteen
pounds?
For the many blessings I have received I will praise the Lord in
thanksgiving
I wonder what the New Year will bring to the world
What changes will we see?
Will humankind find peace?
Will we finally find peace with each other regardless of culture or
religion or skin colour?
Will we stop the destruction of our planet?
Will we?
Will we begin to value life as a precious gift from God?

Is there a chance?

No matter how slim the chance is I hope it happens

Will this be the year that the Dove of Peace will visit our broken and crying world?

Will this be the year?

A FAMILY FRIEND

I still remember her spoken words
I still remember her smiling face
The difficult choices she made without complaint
The quiet space where she often prayed
I remember her loving husband
He is long ago deceased
Her heart remembers his faithful love
Her heart still grieves for him.
I still remember her helping hand
Her special ways will not be forgotten
Her loving touch stays with me still
Her lonely days she filled by doing good deeds.
Her uphill struggle she completed
Her deep secret is now revealed
Her time of trouble is no more
Her aching heart is now healed.
She faced her fears with courage
Her family and friends stayed by her side
Her faith increased day by day
Quietly she waits to hear the Lord's sweet song
She knows now it won't be very long.
Soon she will be going home
Soon she will see her dear husband once more
She has missed his loving arms
Soon she will be crossing over to that other shore.

She celebrated her one hundredth birthday
The Lord guided her footsteps all the way
She died peacefully in her sleep that night
Now she's surrounded by God's Everlasting Light.

LOVE BLOOMS IN JOY

God is good
God is great
God knows all things
He knew when the time was right for us to meet
He knew that we would fall in love
We shared our dreams and conquered our fears
Some of them anyway
We sank our roots into fertile soil
We stretched our limbs with work and our minds with knowledge
We reached out for the sunlight of each new day
We heard the echo of our love song
We felt the warmth of our love as it blossomed in joy.
Our love didn't always blossom in joy
Sometimes it was a slightly faded bloom
Yes, there were tears and there were frowns
There were disagreements
There were times when we wanted to stop the world and get off
Times when we just wanted to disappear into nothingness.
Many years have passed since God brought us together
We've been through calm waters
We've also been through some dangerous rapids
We've survived both sunny days and stormy weather
There have been numerous changes since that wondrous day
Since that day we've left many things behind
We've had many new choices to consider
Memories now come flooding into my head.
I recall times of frustration and desperate worry
Times of grief and sorrow

Times when we had to encourage each other to carry on
To take just one more step
Our love pulled us through
Our faith in each other helped too
Our faith in God gave us the strength we needed
Thank You, Lord!
There were times of awesome wonder and peaceful rest
Times of inspiration
Times of joyful celebrations and family reunions
I remember clearly times of confusion and doubt
Times of severe illness and bouts of dark depression
I wondered if you would survive
I prayed that you would
I praise the Lord that you did.
There were times of hard work
Times when the struggle seemed to be all uphill
Times when we had to rely on God and each other
There were times of learning and times of adventure
We experienced new sights and new sounds.
Then there were times of trouble
Together we got through the trouble
We came out stronger on the other side.
I remember times when we needed an extra helping of patience
Sometimes we needed two or three extra helpings!
Yes, there were times of winding roads and broken dreams
Times of sleepless nights
Times when nothing seemed to go right
There were times of obstacles overcome and goals achieved
There was always love.
At times our love was weak and faded but it was still there

There is still love for us to share

Oh what precious joy!

Oh praise be to God!

Yes, oh yes

They have been years of ups and downs

A perfect mixture of smiles and frowns

The roads of love and life have twisted and turned

They have welcomed and burned

We've loved and we've laughed

We've cried and we've learned

We've achieved some dreams and let others go

We've come a long way

We still have a long way to go.

This is the first day of the New Year

It's a brand new, pristine and untouched year

We will have new challenges to face

Our ideas and attitudes and feelings will flow

Maybe some of them will change

We'll come through it all

We'll come through it all just like we have before

We'll come through it all with the help of God's Grace.

THE EARTHQUAKE

It was an ordinary type of day
Suddenly without warning the ground shook
Buildings trembled then crashed to the ground
Windows shattered
Pavement buckled and cracked
People screamed and ran for their lives
Many were caught beneath the falling rubble
Many would be trapped there for days
Many would die there
Some managed to crawl out.
There was fear
There was confusion
There was weeping
There was praying.
The hours of the night were rapidly approaching
It was dark
It was cold
The few survivors huddled together for warmth
They comforted one another
They shared the few blankets they had
They shared what little food and water they had.
The next day showed the horror and the destruction
Dead bodies were everywhere
Rubble was everywhere
The survivors helped the wounded in whatever ways they could.
Finally the rescue workers arrived
Now the people fought over supplies
People were desperate for clean water.

The days passed
It was now the third day after the earthquake
A child was found under the rubble
He was alive!
It was a moment of joy in the midst of all the sadness
It was a moment of triumph
It was a moment of hope
It gave the people strength to carry on.

THE BOYFRIEND

He showed up at her door one day
He showed up uninvited
She told him to go
He said he had something to tell her
She said she didn't want to know.
This was her boyfriend of long ago
He had already broken her heart
What did he want after all these years?
Did he expect them to make a brand new start?
He gave her a trembling smile
He then made a strange request
He asked her to pray with him
Yes, right here and right now, he said
She gave him a little smile in return
She nodded
How could she refuse?
They held hands and prayed the Lord's Prayer together
What else could she do?
She felt his lips on her forehead
Her fingers touched his cheek
He murmured thank you and then he was gone
He was out of her life again
She wondered why he had tracked her down
She wondered if there was something wrong.
Three days later she read his obituary in the newspaper
She shed a tear for him
She said a prayer for his soul
Then she recalled his short visit

She remembered the pain in his eyes

She no longer wondered why

She knew now that he had come to say goodbye.

I'LL ALWAYS BE HERE FOR YOU

You know I'll always be here for you
You know I'll always care
No matter where we go
No matter what we do
I'm thankful for the love we share.
You know you're very special to me
I know that you know
I'll always be here for you
I know it doesn't always show.
You know I'll always love you
We belong together
Through good times and through bad times we belong together
I know deep down that you love me too
Our love is special
Our love is precious
Our love will stay forever true.

GOODBYE, DAD

It happened
It happened on a cool March evening
It happened three months before his ninety-seventh birthday
It was sad
It was also a blessing
My dear Dad died
He crossed over the river to the other side.
He died at home in his bed
He had been ill for several months
My mother refused to put him in the hospital
No one else was going to care for her man
No one else was going to look after her beloved husband of 67 years
She would do it and she did.
Every day he grew a little weaker
Still she cared for him
On this day my Dad slept a great deal
My mother and I were with him
Suddenly his breathing changed
He opened his eyes and gave us a weak smile
A single tear fell down his cheek
I tenderly wiped it away and whispered goodbye
My mother kissed him for the last time.
For a few seconds my Dad's face seemed to glow
It seemed to glow with a strange light
He closed his eyes as God called his name and led him home.